COUNTRY WALKS AROUND THE NATIONAL FOREST

Brian Conduit

Meridian Books

Published 2007 by Meridian Books

Reprinted 2009

© Brian Conduit 2007

ISBN 978-1-869922-56-6

A catalogue record for this book is available from the British Library.

The right of Brian Conduit to be identified as author of this book has been asserted by him in accordance with the Copyright, Designs and Patents Act 1988.

Meridian Books
40 Hadzor Road, Oldbury, West Midlands B68 9LA

Printed in Great Britain by Cromwell Press Group, Trowbridge, Wiltshire

Contents

Foreword

by Sophie Churchill, Chief Executive,
The National Forest Company

The National Forest is a great place for a walk. Since the early 1990s, there has been an incredible transformation as landowners have joined with us in creating a new forest for the nation across 200 square miles of central England. In a little over 15 years, almost 6,000 hectares of woodland and other habitats have been created and over 7 million trees planted. The result is a rich and vibrant landscape just waiting to be explored. From the ancient woodlands of Charnwood Forest to the floodplains of the River Trent, The National Forest supports an ever-increasing diversity of wildlife. Buzzards, a species once rare in the area, are now a regular sight in the skies over the Forest and otters are returning to our rivers. With all of this new growth and change, it would be easy to forget the past. But, with wonderful stately homes such as Calke Abbey and fascinating industrial museums like Sharpe's Pottery Centre, the varied human history of the Forest is being preserved and presented for future generations to enjoy.

The twenty walks in this book are a marvellous introduction to The National Forest and its surrounding area. They will take you through sleepy villages and bustling towns, wooded hills and rolling farmland. As a resident of the Forest, I know that this guide will help me appreciate its variety all the more. Whether you live here or are visiting, I am sure that you will enjoy these walks and I hope that you will come back to explore all that The National Forest has to offer.

Sophie Churchill

Introduction

A landscape is not a static phenomenon. Landscapes are evolving all the time, some more than others. The National Forest is changing quicker than most and in its fairly short life – little more than a decade – those changes are already apparent. But what is The National Forest and where exactly is it? These are undoubtedly the most commonly asked questions by people from outside the area.

Its geographical location is straightforward enough. It extends over roughly 200 square miles of east Staffordshire, south Derbyshire and west Leicestershire within an area bounded by the large cities of Stoke-on-Trent, Derby, Nottingham, Leicester and Birmingham. Within its borders are four main towns – Burton upon Trent, Swadlincote, Ashby-de-la-Zouch and Coalville – villages and smaller towns, historic sites, mature woodland, new plantations, parkland, farmland and a former coalfield area. The River Trent winds across the heart of it and for much of the way it is partnered – and occasionally joined – by the Trent and Mersey Canal. Both waterways provide much attractive walking.

The previous paragraph reveals that The National Forest is more than just an area of woodland but this is nothing new. Contrary to popular belief, this was true of the larger forests that in the Middle Ages covered around a third of the country. But the primary aim behind The National Forest project is to increase the tree cover in the area to around 33% and provide a patchwork of woods in what had become one of the least wooded parts of the country. Over the last few centuries many of the trees had been lost as a result of agricultural encroachment, industrial development, urban growth and the demands of two world wars.

As the newly planted woodlands grow and become merged with each other, they will ultimately create a physical link between the two medieval forests whose remains occupy the western and eastern fringes of the area. These are the forests of Needwood and Charnwood respectively. In the Middle Ages Needwood in east Staffordshire was a royal hunting forest, part of the Duchy of Lancaster, and covered most of the area roughly between Uttoxeter, Tutbury and Lichfield. It was very thickly wooded and noted for its fine oaks but from the eighteenth century onwards most of it was felled. Charnwood in west Leicestershire was never a royal forest but a chase, sometimes referred to as Charley Chase, whose hunting rights were owned jointly between various earls and local religious houses. It covered an area roughly between Leicester, Loughborough and Coalville but, unlike Needwood, was never thickly wooded. Much of its lower land comprised rough heath and the higher slopes – and Charnwood is a hilly region rising to over 900 feet – were and still are characterised by fern and gorse interspersed with craggy outcrops.

Another aim of The National Forest is to regenerate areas of industrial decline and dereliction and make them green and attractive again. Part of the region, around Ashby-de-la-Zouch and Coalville, became a coal mining area and a number of pits were sunk in the early nineteenth century. The mines and many of the ancillary industries have all closed down and since the creation of The National Forest, derelict industrial sites have been restored, coal waste has been landscaped and trees planted to create attractive recreational areas of wood, grassland and water. Visits to Donisthorpe Woodland Park near Ashby, Sence Valley Forest Park just to the south west of Coalville and the area around Thornton Reservoir vividly illustrate how much the landscape has been transformed in a remarkably short time.

This walking guide is not just confined to the boundaries of The National Forest but also includes a number of interesting and attractive areas on its periphery. As with many parts of the country outside the national parks and other obvious honeypot tourist destinations, this is very much an understated and underrated area. The landscape is pleasant and undulating rather than spectacular, although there are plenty of extensive, sweeping and even dramatic views from some of the higher points in Needwood and Charnwood forests looking across the valleys of the Trent and some of its tributaries. A number of great parklands are dotted throughout the area – Bradgate, Melbourne, Staunton Harold and Calke – and these provide superb walking facilities, as well as the intrinsic historic appeal of the great houses themselves and their attendant churches. The many woodlands, both new and mature, are obviously among the major attractions for walkers as are paths across riverside meadows and canal towpaths. In addition there are attractive villages, perhaps less well-known and commercialised than their counterparts in many other parts of the country, and many sites of historic interest, most of which are featured in the selection of walks.

The extensive network of generally clear and well waymarked public rights of way is supplemented by a number of permissive paths created by – among others – the Staunton Harold Estate, National Trust and Severn Trent Water. Also there is public access to all the new woodlands planted through The National Forest scheme.

The forests and chases of the past were the private preserves of monarchs and aristocrats. The National Forest is an evolving forest, a forest for the present and future, a forest that can be enjoyed by all. And the finest way to enjoy and appreciate it is on foot.

Brian Conduit
Clitheroe, 2007

The Routes

None of the walks are strenuous and are well within the capabilities of almost all walkers, including children, although notice that their lengths vary. All are on public rights of way or permissive routes, such as paths across National Trust land, Forestry Commission paths and canal towpaths. Road walking is kept to a minimum and is mainly confined to quiet country lanes. Where stretches of main road are unavoidable, there is always a pavement or grass verge.

Every effort has been made to ensure that descriptions are correct and the routes have been carefully checked. However, no guarantee can be given that they are error free and that there are no misprints or inaccuracies.

The routes should be easy to follow, although you are advised to take with you the appropriate Ordnance Survey Explorer map. If while on a public footpath you encounter obstacles which make your passage difficult, report any such problems to the Rights of Way department of the relevant local authority (addresses below).

Maps

The sketch maps are intended as a guide, not to replace Ordnance Survey maps which, together with a compass and some basic first aid, you should always have with you. Although I hope this will not happen, there is always the possibility that you might need to change your route because of bad weather or some unexpected incident. Maps should preferably be the Explorer series which are much more useful to walkers than Landrangers.

Explorer 245 (The National Forest) covers the vast majority of the walks in this guide, 17 out of the 20. The other three are covered by Explorers 232 (Nuneaton & Tamworth), 246 (Loughborough) and 260 (Nottingham).

Useful addresses and websites

The National Forest Company, Bath Yard, Moira, Swadlincote, Derbyshire DE12 6BD
Tel: 01283 551211 www.nationalforest.org

The Ramblers' Association, 2nd Floor, Camelford House, 87-90 Albert Embankment , London SE1 7TW
Tel: 020 7339 8500. www.ramblers.org.uk

The National Trust, PO Box 39, Warrington WA5 7WD
Tel: 0870 458 4000. www.nationaltrust.org.uk

Local Authorities:

Staffordshire County Council, County Buildings, Martin Street, Stafford ST16 2LH
Tel: 01785 223121. www.staffordshire.gov.uk

Derbyshire County Council, County Hall, Matlock, Derbyshire DE4 3AG
Tel: 0845 605 8058. www.derbyshire.gov.uk

Leicestershire County Council, County Hall, Glenfield, Leicester LE3 8RA
Tel: 0116 232 3232. www.leics.gov.uk

Local Tourist Information Centres:

North Street, Ashby-de-Zouch, Leicestershire LE65 1HU
Tel: 01530 411767. www.nwleicestershire.gov.uk

Coors Visitor Centre, Horninglow Street, Burton upon Trent, Staffordshire
DE14 1NG Tel: 01283 508111. www.enjoyeaststaffs.gov.uk

Sharpe's Pottery Museum, West Street, Swadlincote, Derbyshire DE11
9DG
Tel: 01283 222848. www.south-derbys.gov.uk/tourism

Public Transport

For information about bus and train services either phone Traveline on
0870 6082608 or visit the website. www.traveline.org.uk. Alternatively
contact the local tourist information centre.

About the author

Brian Conduit was born and bred in Birmingham, went to school there
and obtained a B.A.Hons. degree in Medieval and Modern History
from Birmingham University in 1960. He became a history teacher,
first in Buckinghamshire but mainly in Lancashire where he has have lived for
over 40 years, although still retaining many connections with the Midlands.
While teaching in Lancashire he began writing walking guides and after taking
early retirement in 1995 concentrated full time on writing. For many years he
has been Series Consultant and principal author of the Pathfinder walking
guides, published by Jarrold.

He has written over 40 books, plus articles on history and walking for
History Today, The Great Outdoors, Footloose, Outdoor and *Country
Walking*. He has also presented five series of walking programmes, *Walking
through History*, on Radio Lancashire 1984-89.

Also by the author:

Walking through History (Constable 1983)

Exploring Sherwood Forest (Dalesman 1985)

Walks from your Car – Sherwood Forest (Dalesman 1988)

Heritage Trails in North West England (Cicerone 1989)

Walking in Warwickshire (Cicerone 1998)

Discovery Walks in Lancashire (Sigma 1999)

Discovery Walks in Worcestershire (Sigma 2000)

Discovery Walks in Birmingham and the Black Country (Sigma 2001)

Battlefield Walks in the Midlands (Sigma 2004)

Battlefield Walks: Northumbria and the Scottish Borders (Sigma 2005)

Short Walks – Sussex and South Downs (Jarrold 2003)

Short Walks – South Devon (Jarrold 2004)

Walks into History: Lancashire (Countryside 2006)

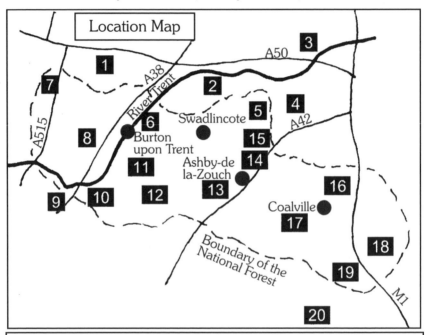

Publisher's Note

Every care has been taken in the preparation of this book. All the walks have been carefully checked and are believed to be correct at the time of publication. However, neither the author or the publishers can accept responsibility for any errors or omissions or for any loss, damage, injury or inconvenience resulting from the use of this book.

Please remember that the countryside is continually changing: hedges and fences may be removed or re-sited; landmarks may disappear; footpaths may be re-routed or be ploughed over and not reinstated (as the law requires); concessionary paths may be closed.

1

A Queen's Prison, and a Wartime Disaster

Tutbury, Stonepit Hills and Hanbury

From the higher points on the route there are striking and extensive views across the Dove and Trent valleys and over the wooded slopes of Needwood Forest. There is also a variety of historic interest that includes the impressive Norman castle and priory at Tutbury, restored medieval church at Hanbury and the enormous crater near Hanbury that resulted from a mystery explosion during the Second World War.

Distance: 7 miles/11.3km.
Approximate time: 3½ hours.
Start: Tutbury, top end of High Street (GR SK213288).
Maps: Explorer 245; Landranger 128.
Car Parking: Free car parks at Tutbury.
Public Transport: Buses from Burton-on-Trent, Derby and Uttoxeter.
Terrain: Riverside meadows, field paths and woodland; two modest climbs. Less agile walkers should know that there are around 26 stiles to negotiate.
Refreshments: Pubs and cafes at Tutbury, tea room at Tutbury Castle, pub at Hanbury.
Public Toilets: Tutbury.

T*he former glass making village of Tutbury is dominated by the extensive ruins of the Norman castle which crown a long ridge above the Dove Valley. The castle was first built in the late eleventh century and extensively rebuilt in the twelfth century. In 1265 it became part of the Duchy of Lancaster and John of Gaunt, son of Edward III, added some walls and towers in the fourteenth century. Between 1569 and 1587 it served as the prison for Mary, Queen of Scots who hated the place, complaining that it was cold and damp. The castle fell into ruin after the Civil War and the Great Hall is the only part that has a roof and is still intact. The tower on the motte is a folly, added in the eighteenth century.*

Just below the castle is the former Benedictine priory. Tutbury was one of a number of alien priories in England, which means that it was a dependency of a continental monastery, in this case an abbey in Normandy. It was dissolved by Henry VIII in 1537 and all that remains is the fine Norman church, now the parish church, much reduced in size.

Facing High Street ❶ turn left along Duke Street and continue uphill along Castle Street. At a public footpath sign just after the road bends left, turn right along an enclosed path. Immediately there is a striking view ahead over the Dove Valley. Descend a flight of steps, go through a kissing gate, continue down beside the castle mound on the right and keep straight ahead across a meadow.

On the far side bear right through a hedge gap and turn left over a stile. Walk across a field, climb two stiles in quick succession and bear left across the corner of the next field to climb another stile. Maintain the same direction across a meadow – the River Dove is just to the right – keeping to the left of a ruined barn and gradually veering left to a stile at a hedge corner. Climb it and another one, walk along a left field edge and climb two more stiles in quick succession. Continue along the right edge of a field to a track, turn left over a stile and turn right to a road.

Turn right and at a public footpath sign, turn left ❷ along a tarmac drive through Fauld Industrial Park. Bear right and at the end of the park, turn right over a stile. Walk along the right edge of a field, climb a stile in the corner and turn left onto an enclosed path. Climb a stile, bear right through a gate, continue along an enclosed path and climb another stile. Bear slightly right and head quite steeply uphill over the Stonepit Hills, keeping to the left of the trees, to reach the brow. This is a magnificent viewpoint over Needwood Forest and the Trent and Dove valleys, with the hills of the Peak District visible on the horizon.

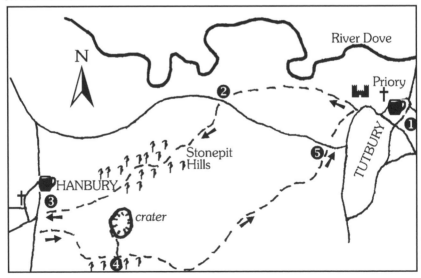

Tutbury Castle

From the brow follow a line of waymarked posts over bumpy ground to a stile on the edge of Queen's Purse Wood. Climb it and continue along a winding fence-lined path through this beautiful woodland to reach a track. Turn right, follow the track as it curves left and at a fork, keep along the left hand track. Where this track bends right, keep ahead along a grassy path, passing several notices on the left with warnings about unexploded bombs and steep drops. This indicates that you are near the edge of the crater but more about this later.

Climb steps and go through a kissing gate on the edge of the woodland. Walk along the right edge of the next two fields but in the second field veer left away from the edge to go through a kissing gate. Continue along an enclosed path, go through a gate, almost immediately turn left through a kissing gate, turn right and head across to a stile beside a gate. After climbing it, walk along an enclosed track and go through a kissing gate onto a road in the village of Hanbury. The Cock Inn is to the right but you turn left to a T-junction. **❸**

The pleasant village of Hanbury has fine views over the Dove Valley and Needwood Forest. The medieval church was extensively restored and partially rebuilt in the nineteenth century. It has a memorial window to the 1944 disaster.

Turn left, in the Anslow and Burton direction, and at a public footpath sign to the Crater, turn left along an enclosed track to a kissing gate. Go through and as you continue along the track ahead, passing through two kissing gates, grand and extensive views open up over the Trent valley. After the second kissing gate, continue along the right edge of a field, in the corner turn left to keep along the field edge and go through a kissing gate. **❹**

The main route continues ahead but turn left along the left edge of the field for a short detour to the crater. Go through a kissing gate, keep along the edge of the next field, go through another kissing gate and keep ahead through bushes to the crater, bearing left by a wire fence on the right in order to get a good view.

On the morning of 27 November 1944 a huge explosion at a large RAF ammunitions dump of over 4000 tons of explosives, stored in former gypsum mines here, rocked the surrounding area. Over 70 people were killed, a local farm was destroyed and there was much damage in nearby Hanbury, including the Cock Inn. The cause of the explosion remains a mystery to this day but it is one of the largest ever non-nuclear explosions. The enormous crater left behind is approximately 1000 yards long and 300 yards wide.

Trent Valley from the Stonepit Hills

Retrace your steps to the main route ④ and turn left to head across the field. After going over a low brow, veer right, making for a hedge corner, and keep ahead by a hedge and wire fence on the left. Look out for where you turn left over a footbridge and stile and turn right to continue along the right field edge. Approaching the corner, bear left to climb a stile, keep along the left edge of the next field and climb two stiles in quick succession.

Walk along the left edge of a field, bear left to climb two stiles in quick succession and continue along the left edge of the next field towards a farm. Keep ahead to the farm buildings, bending first right and then left to pass to the left of them, and at a fork take the right hand track. At a public footpath sign where the track bends right, keep ahead across a field, making for the far right hand corner where you join a track.

For the remainder of the walk you enjoy dramatic views of Tutbury's hilltop castle getting gradually closer.

Bear left, walk along the right edge of a field and just after the field edge curves left, look out for where you turn right over a stile. Turn left to continue along a left field edge and follow the edge around a right bend. Turn left over a stile, turn right along a right field edge, cross a plank footbridge into the next field and turn left along its left edge. At a junction of paths by a footpath post, turn left through a hedge gap, cross another plank footbridge and walk along the right edge of a field to a road. ❺

Cross over, take the path opposite to the left of a house and climb a stile. Walk along the left field edge, later curving right and ascending the slopes to go through a hedge gap just below the top of the ridge. Continue up to climb a stile, head up to climb another one and turn left along a narrow enclosed path. On reaching the top of steps on the left, turn right, here picking up the outward route, and retrace your steps to the start.

2

Mercia's Ancient Capital

Repton and Newton Solney

Between Repton and Newton Solney there is attractive riverside walking beside the Trent, passing its confluence with the Dove. On the return stretch you leave the river to climb gently above the valley and are rewarded with some superb and extensive views across gently rolling countryside, with the spire of Repton church prominent.

Distance: 5 miles/8km.
Approximate time: 2½ hours.
Start: Repton, Market Cross (GRSK304270).
Maps: Explorer 245; Landranger 128.
Car Parking: Free car parks at Repton.
Public Transport: Buses from Derby and Burton upon Trent.
Terrain: Easy walking across fields and riverside meadows: about 16 stiles.
Refreshments: Pubs and café at Repton, pubs at Newton Solney.
Public Toilets: Repton.

For a short while Repton was the capital of Mercia and its church the burial place of Mercian kings. The town has quite a complicated ecclesiastical history. The church was founded in AD653 and an adjacent monastery established shortly afterwards. It was sacked by the Danes in the winter of AD873-4 but the eighth century crypt, intended to be the mausoleum of the Mercian kings, survived and lies under the present church which was built later on the monastic site. This church was substantially enlarged between the thirteenth and fifteenth centuries and the impressive tower and spire, 212 feet high and a landmark for miles around, dates from the fifteenth century.

A Benedictine priory was founded around 1172 next to the church and the former Saxon monastery. This was dissolved by Henry VIII in the 1530s and a school was founded on its site in the reign of Elizabeth I. The arch from this former priory now forms the entrance to some of the school buildings. Repton School totally dominates this small and unassuming town as almost every other building seems to be connected with it.

Facing the church ❶, walk along the main road and follow it around left and right bends. Just after the right bend, turn left along a track to a public

Pleasant Countryside near Repton

footpath sign and continue along a straight tarmac path, by a hedge on the right, to a lane. Cross it and keep ahead along an enclosed path to a stile.

Climb it, head diagonally across an uneven narrow field, keep along its left edge to a hedge corner and continue across the field to climb a stile in the right hand corner. Keep ahead, by a hedge on the left and above a wooded hollow

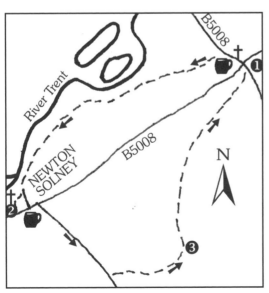

on the right, and follow the path to a stile. After climbing it, keep along the right field edge for about 50 yards (46m), turn right over a stile and turn left to continue along the left inside edge of woodland that slopes down to the River Trent.

Go through a gate, keep ahead by the river and the path curves right through a hedge gap. Immediately turn left initially by the left edge of a meadow, later continuing across it to a stile in a fence in the far right hand corner. Climb it, keep ahead in the same direction across a field, climb another stile and head across the next field to a stile. After climbing it, continue diagonally across the next field, making for the corner of a hedge on the left. Keep ahead to join the riverbank again just about at the point where the Dove flows into the Trent. Climb a stile and head across to a track. Follow this sunken, tree-lined track around a left bend and it becomes a tarmac lane. When you see steps on the right, climb them, walk along a path and go through a kissing gate into the churchyard at Newton Solney.

The small village of Newton Solney occupies a delightful situation near the confluence of the Trent and Dove. Its fine medieval church was founded in the twelfth century but mainly dates from the fourteenth and fifteenth centuries. There are some attractive Victorian almshouses in the main street.

Meeting of the rivers Trent and Dove near Newton Solney

Go through another kissing gate, turn left along a drive to a road **2** and turn left again into the village. Take the first road on the right (Newton Lane, Bretby Lane), ignore the first public footpath sign on the left but at the second one, turn left along a tarmac, fence-lined drive. In front of the gates to a house, turn left through a gate, walk along the right field edge and climb a stile beside a gate. Walk across a field, go through a gate, bear right and head gently uphill to a stile. Climb it, turn left along the left field edge and climb another stile. Keep ahead across a field, passing to the left of a tree that marks an old hedge line, and about half-way across the next field, look out for a path on the left **3** and follow it in a straight line to a stile.

Climb it, bear right to head across a large field, climb another stile on the far side, continue across the next field and go through a gate onto an enclosed track. Turn right and at a T-junction of tracks, keep ahead over a stile and walk across a field. Climb a stile in the corner, keep along the left edge of two fields, head straight across the next field and continue along an enclosed path to a road on the edge of Repton.

Cross it, take the enclosed path opposite and follow it around a right bend to a stile. Climb it, keep along the enclosed path and pass beside a gate onto another road. Continue along an enclosed path and at a fork, take the left hand path to emerge onto a road. Turn right to the Market Cross.

A Meeting of Three Waterways

Shardlow, Church Wilne and Derwent Mouth

The emphasis on this walk is very much on water. It starts at a fascinating former canal port and takes you to the meeting place of three waterways: the rivers Trent and Derwent and the Trent and Mersey Canal. The lack of a footbridge over the canal at Derwent Mouth Lock means that there has to be much retracing of steps but that is not a problem as the wide views across the adjacent meadows are a more than adequate bonus and a visit to an isolated medieval church adds to the interest.

Distance: 5 miles/8km
Approximate time: 2½ hours
Start: Shardlow, Wharf car park (GRSK445305)
Maps: Explorer 260; Landranger 129.
Car Parking: Shardlow Wharf car park (free)
Public Transport: Buses from Derby, Loughborough and Castle Donington
Terrain: Flat walking along lanes, across meadows and on a canal towpath
Refreshments: Pubs at Shardlow
Public toilets: None

Turn right out of the car park ❶ along the lane, cross the canal bridge and follow the lane into the hamlet of Great Wilne. Where the lane ends, climb a stile and turn right to follow a worn path by the right edge of a field. At the far end of the field, cross a footbridge over the River Derwent, turn left beside the river and the path emerges onto a lane.

Turn left and at a public footpath sign, turn right, walk across a field and climb a stile. Continue along the right edge of the next field to a lane and turn right to the church at Church Wilne. ❷

The highly atmospheric church of St Chad stands in isolation on low lying land that has always been prone to flooding, hence the virtual disappearance of the village. The church dates back to the Middle Ages but had to be almost completely rebuilt after being gutted by a fire in 1917. Across the road is St Chad's Water, a local nature reserve reclaimed since 1984 from gravel workings.

Isolated medieval church at Church Wilne

Retrace your steps to the canal bridge at Shardlow and immediately after crossing it, turn left to join the towpath of the Trent and Mersey Canal. Follow it, passing a marina on the left, to Derwent Mouth Lock and on for another quarter of a mile (400m) to Derwent Mouth. ❸

Derwent Mouth is the meeting place of three waterways. Here both the River Derwent and the Trent and Mersey Canal flow into the River Trent. Downstream a viaduct takes the M1 motorway over the Trent.

Retrace your steps along the towpath to Shardlow, going under the road bridge that you previously crossed, no 4. Continue past canalside pubs, moorings and restored warehouses to the next road bridge where you go up to the road. Turn right and cross the bridge to the imposing Clock Warehouse and nearby Heritage Centre.

Situated near the confluence of the rivers Trent and Derwent, the small river port of Shardlow grew rapidly after the opening of the Trent and Mersey Canal in 1777. The canal was constructed to link the Trent with the River Mersey at Runcorn in Cheshire, a distance of about 93 miles (149km).

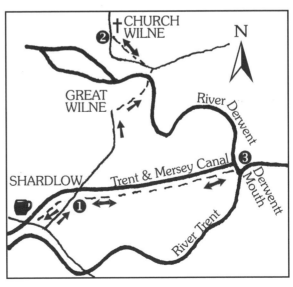

The decline of the canals led to Shardlow becoming almost derelict by the 1970s but since then conservation and restoration has led to its revival and there has been greater recognition of its unique place in our history. It is a rare and fascinating example of an eighteenth century canal port with warehouses, wharves, workshops, cottages and houses, stables, boat building yards and other buildings associated with the canal trade at that time. Particularly impressive is the Clock Warehouse, built in 1780 and now a pub. It is so called because a clock once adorned the front of the building. The nearby Heritage Centre is housed in the oldest warehouse in the village and well worth a visit.

Return over the bridge, keep ahead and take the first turning on the left (Wilne Lane) to return to the start.

Meeting place of the rivers Trent and Mersey and the Trent & Mersey Canal at Derwent Mouth

Fine Views and Outstanding Churches

Melbourne and Breedon on the Hill

There is much pleasant and easy walking across fields and through parkland with fine views over the surrounding countryside. The full walk includes a climb to the top of Breedon Hill, well worth the effort and the extra distance both for the magnificent view and the interesting church, whose tower can be seen for miles around. The final stretch beside The Pool, passing Melbourne Hall and the adjacent and exceptionally imposing Norman church, is particularly attractive.

Distance: 6 miles/9.7km for the full walk; 5 miles/8km for the shorter version.
Approximate time: 3 hours for the full walk; 2½ hours for the shorter walk.
Start: Melbourne, Market Place (GR SK386253).
Maps: Explorer 245; Landranger 128.
Car Parking: Free car parks at Melbourne.
Public Transport: Buses from Derby, Nottingham and Swadlincote.
Terrain: Field paths and tracks through gently rolling country, one climb if doing the full walk.
Refreshments: Pubs and cafes at Melbourne, pub at Wilson, pub at Breedon on the Hill, tea room at Melbourne Hall.
Public Toilets: Melbourne.

Melbourne was once a centre for framework knitting and footwear manufacturing and possesses a number of attractive, brick-built Georgian and Victorian buildings. One of its most famous citizens was Thomas Cook, founder of the travel company, who was born here in 1808.

❶ Start by walking along Church Street, passing to the left of the church, and the road continues as Blackwell Lane. At a public footpath sign, turn right through a kissing gate and walk across grass. Bear slightly right to keep by the edge of woodland on the right and then bear left and head diagonally across the field between widely-spaced trees, looking for a stile in a hedge.

Climb it, continue across the next field to a track on the far left hand side and turn left beside a cattle grid. Bear left to climb a stile, continue gently uphill along the left field edge and climb a stile on the brow. From here there are superb all round views. Bear slightly left and as you head downhill across the next field, Breedon's hilltop church can be seen over to the right. The path emerges onto a road on the edge of the village of Wilson. The Bulls Head is a few yards to the left but the route continues to the right along a tarmac drive called Green Lane.

Here the shorter and longer walks separate. For the longer walk continue reading from ✱ below.

Followng the shorter walk (that omits Breedon on the Hill) continue along the drive which narrows after passing a golf club car park. Where the drive bends right, turn left along a track and follow it around a right bend. Keep along the right edge of fields, by a hedge on the right. Eventually the track bends right through a gap in the hedge and then turns left to continue along the left field edge. Where the field edge curves right at a fingerpost, keep ahead through a hedge gap and walk along the right edge of part of the golf course to another hedge gap. ❹ This is where you rejoin the full walk. Now continue reading from ✪ on page 26.

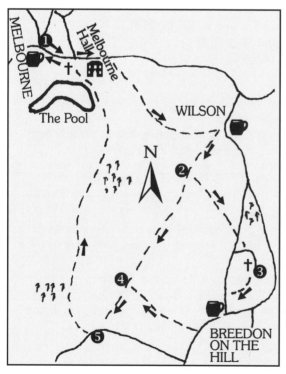

✱ Continuing the full walk, turn left through a hedge gap at a public footpath sign ❷ and keep in a straight line across a golf course. There are several waymarked posts to show the way. Nearing the far end of the course, bear right across to the right edge and continue along a track under an avenue of trees. Where the track curves right, climb a stile onto a narrow lane and take the path opposite. The path initially runs parallel to the lane but later bears left away from it and climbs steeply through trees to a lane. Turn left

The line of the walk near Melbourne

and the lane curves right to the church at Breedon on the Hill. ❸

The isolated limestone bulk of Breedon Hill towers 400 feet (122m) above the surrounding countryside. The views are magnificent, extending over Charnwood Forest and the Trent Valley to the cities of Derby and Nottingham. In clear conditions, the southern fringes of the Peak District are visible on the northern horizon. Much of the eastern half of the hill has disappeared as a result of extensive quarrying activities.

The site is an ancient site with evidence of an Iron Age fort. In the seventh century a Saxon monastery was founded here. This was largely destroyed by the Danes during their conquest of Mercia but the Saxon heritage survives through the extensive collection of carvings built into the walls of the later medieval priory. Particularly impressive is the Breedon Angel, one of the earliest and finest surviving examples of Saxon sculpture. The priory was dissolved by Henry VIII in the 1530s and the present church is basically the tower and east end of that priory, purchased for the local people as their parish church by Francis Shirley of the nearby Staunton Harold Hall. The west end of the former priory was demolished because it was in such a bad state. As well as the Saxon carvings, the church contains some fine tombs of the Shirley family.

Where the lane ends, keep ahead through a gate and walk along an enclosed path which descends via steps to reach a road in Breedon village. Bear right to a T-junction, turn left and where the road divides, take the right hand road across the green and keep ahead along the main road. At a public footpath sign, turn right onto a path through trees which curves left and then bends right to continue as a straight, hedge-lined grassy track.

Continue by a hedge on the left, go through a hedge gap and head gently uphill by a hedge on the left. Follow the field edge around first a right bend and then a left bend and continue over the brow of the hill. In the field corner follow the edge to the right and at a waymarked post, turn left to descend into a dip and go through a hedge gap into a field. Turn left and follow the field edge to the right to a yellow waymark by another hedge gap. ❹

Turn left through it, here meeting the shorter route.

✪The route continues first along an enclosed path and then along a right field edge, following the edge around right and left bends and passing beside a gate onto a lane. Turn right and at a public footpath sign, turn right over a stile, ❺ walk across a field and climb a waymarked stile in a fence. Bear right downhill across a sloping field, climb a double stile in the bottom right hand corner and turn right, passing a waymarked post. Climb a stile and walk along a path, later by the right edge of woodland, climbing a series of stiles to reach a gate. Go through, keep ahead through an avenue of trees and on approaching the next gate the tower of Melbourne church comes into view.

Go through the gate – here the track bends left towards a farm – and keep ahead gently downhill, by a wire fence on the right, bending right to climb a stile in the field corner. Climb steps, walk along the right edge of the next field and where the edge curves right, keep ahead and climb another stile. Continue across a field to a stile in a hedge, climb it, head across the next field and go through a kissing gate.

Turn left along a tarmac track for a most attractive finale along the right edge of The Pool and past Melbourne Hall and church to a road.

Melbourne church is unusually imposing for a small place, cathedral-like in dimensions and appearance and an outstanding example of Norman architecture. The most plausible reason for this is that it was originally a royal foundation, built by Henry I around 1120. In 1133 it was given by the king to the newly created bishopric of Carlisle. Almost the whole of the building dates from the early twelfth century except for part of the chancel, rebuilt in the fifteenth century, and the upper part of the central tower, probably added in the early seventeenth century.

The adjacent hall was originally the rectory for the medieval bishops of Carlisle. It later came into the possession of the Coke family and was mostly rebuilt by them in the late seventeenth and early eighteenth centuries. The magnificent formal gardens were laid out at roughly the same time. During the first half of the nineteenth century it was the home of Lord Melbourne, Queen Victoria's first Prime Minister, after whom the city of Melbourne in Australia is named.

At the road turn left to return to the Market Place.

A Baroque Mansion in Decline

Calke Park and Ticknall

The first and last parts of this outstanding walk give you attractive views over Staunton Harold Reservoir. In between you stroll across the delightful parkland surrounding Calke Abbey, enjoying a grand view of the house, to the village of Ticknall. The route then takes you across fields and along the edge of both mature and newer woodlands before returning to the start.

Distance: 8 miles/12.9km
Approximate time: 4 hours.
Start: Visitor Centre at northern end of Staunton Harold Reservoir, signposted from Melbourne, GRSK377245.
Maps: Explorer 245; Landranger 128.
Car Parking: Severn Trent Water pay car park at Staunton Harold Reservoir.
Public Transport: None, but you could start the walk from Ticknall which is served by buses from Nottingham, Swadlincote and Melbourne.
Terrain: Gentle walking through woodland and across fields and parkland; there are twenty stiles to negotiate!.
Refreshments: Kiosk at start (opening times vary), tea room at Calke Abbey, pubs at Ticknall.
Public Toilets: At start.

S taunton Harold Reservoir was created in 1964 and extends over an area of 209 acres It has become an important wildlife habitat and a popular centre for water sports, fishing, bird watching, cycling and walking. The Windmill Tower which overlooks the reservoir was used for the milling of local grain. It was built in 1798 but had become derelict by the end of the nineteenth century.There is an information room at the visitor centre.

Begin ❶ by walking up to the Windmill Tower, pass to the left of it and at a public footpath sign, go through a fence gap and bear left across a field. Continue along the right edge of the next two fields, then along the left edge of the third field and keep ahead across the fourth field. On the far side of this field turn right to continue along its left edge and climb a stile in the corner.

Keep ahead along an enclosed path by the left inside edge of trees, climb a stile and walk along a left field edge. Climb a stile, continue across a field,

In Calke Park

climb another stile, continue across the next field and climb a stile onto a lane. Cross over, climb the stile opposite and head down across a field to cross a footbridge. Keep ahead uphill across the next field and on the far side, turn left along the right field edge. Continue along an enclosed path, re-entering the field, and walk across the corner of it to a stile.

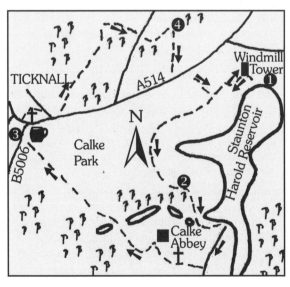

Climb it, cross a track, keep ahead across the next field and climb a stile in the corner. Keep ahead along the eight edge of the next field but soon turn right through a gate to enter Calke Park. ❷ Turn left along the left inside edge of woodland, climb a stile and continue beside the fence of a deer enclosure on the right. The path bends right, gently descends and continues through woodland to cross a footbridge over

The elegant facade of Calke Abbey

an arm of Staunton Harold Reservoir. Turn left across another footbridge and continue by the reservoir, crossing another footbridge.

The path eventually turns right away from the water and heads up to emerge onto a lane by a car park. From here there is a superb view looking towards the starting point at the northern end of the reservoir. Keep ahead along the lane and on the edge of Calke village, turn right along a tarmac drive. You pass to the left of the church and drop into a dip from where you get a magnificent view of the façade of the great house.

The splendid Baroque mansion of Calke Abbey has been described as a vivid example of the decline of the English country house. This is because its faded splendours illustrate a house that has changed little since the 1880s.

There was originally a medieval priory on the site and later an Elizabethan mansion. Sir John Harpur built the present house between 1701 and 1704. Some of the Harpurs were renowned for their eccentricity, in particular an obsession with natural history, and the house reflects this, containing an extensive collection of hunting trophies, stuffed animals and other curiosities. It also possesses an unusual eighteenth century bed. The superb restored orangery and fine walled gardens are well worth a visit and the magnificent parkland, over 600 acres in area, is renowned for its ancient oaks, pastures, deer enclosure and pools.

In the nearby church, built in 1826, there is a monument to Sir John Harpur and his wife.

Continue along the drive to the outbuildings of the house. These include the stable block, tearoom and an information centre where you purchase tickets to visit the house, gardens and church. The walk continues to the left along a drive across open parkland. In front of a gate, follow the drive to the right, pass the end of Mere Pond, go through a gate and continue along the drive to a lodge. After passing under an arch by the lodge, turn left by a fence bordering woodland and when you see a stile on the left, turn right onto a grassy path and continue across the parkland. After climbing a stile, keep ahead across two fields and continue along the left edge of the second field to climb a stile and keep ahead to a road in Ticknall. ❸

The attractive and now quiet estate village of Ticknall was once a busy hive of industry with limestone quarrying and brick making activities. Its church dates from 1842 but fragments of its medieval successor survive in the churchyard.

Turn right to a T-junction, turn left and at a public footpath sign, turn right through a gate and walk along a path by a wall on the right to a stile. The churchyard is to the right. Climb the stile, continue along the right edge of a playing field, climb another stile in the corner and turn right along the right field edge. Go through a kissing gate, keep along the right edge of the next field and go through another kissing gate into the car park of the village hall. This could be an alternative starting point for the walk, especially for those using public transport. Walk across the car park and continue along a path to go through a gate onto a road. Turn right to a T-junction and turn left to continue along the main road through the village.

Ahead is an arch across the road. This is the Tramway Bridge, built in 1802 to carry a tramway that ran from the quarries and brickworks of Ticknall to the Ashby Canal at Willesley.

At a public bridleway sign to Ingleby, turn left across a grassy area to a gate. Go through, walk across a field, go through another gate and bear right across a field corner to a stile. Climb it and continue in the same direction across the next field, skirting the left edge of trees and making for a stile in a hedge near the field corner. After climbing it, keep ahead by a fence bordering a new plantation on the left and climb a stile onto a track.

Cross it, walk across a field and continue on a path that keeps by the right inside edge of the delightful woodland of Gorsey Leys. To the right is the new plantation of Vees Wood. At a T-junction, turn right beside a gate and walk along an enclosed path, continuing along a left field edge to a road. Cross over and take the path ahead along the right edge of a field. Over to the right is Nut Wood, another new plantation and more evidence of the continuous expansion of The National Forest. The field edge bends left to emerge onto a track by St Brides Farm. ❹

Turn right through a gate, walk along a hedge-lined path, go through another gate and keep ahead. The path widens into a track to emerge onto a road. Turn left and turn right along a track called Bog Lane. Immediately in front is a view of Staunton Harold Reservoir and the tower of Breedon church can be seen on the skyline. Where the track ends, climb a stile and turn left along the left edge of a field. Here you pick up the outward route and retrace your steps to the start.

A Rural Walk in a Town Centre

Burton-upon-Trent

For a short walk in the middle of a busy town this one is hard to beat. The views across the Washlands, the flood plain of the River Trent, are superb and both the flower beds at Stapenhill Gardens and the tree-lined riverside paths are exceptionally attractive. A brief foray into the town centre of Burton to St Modwen's church and the Market Place provides a contrast with the rest of the walk.

Distance: 2½ miles/4km.
Approximate time: 1½ hours.
Start: Burton upon Trent, Stapenhill Road car park
(GR SK255224).
Maps: Explorer 245; Landranger 128.
Car Parking: Stapenhill Road car park off the A444 on the east side of the River Trent. There are plenty of other car parks close to the walk which could be used, especially the Meadowside car park on the west side of the river just to the south of Burton Bridge.
Public Transport: Buses from Uttoxeter, Swadlincote, Ashby-de-la-Zouch, Birmingham, Lichfield and Derby; trains from Birmingham, Tamworth and Derby.
Terrain: Easy and flat walking mostly on tarmac riverside paths.
Refreshments: Plenty of pubs and cafés at Burton upon Trent.
Public Toilets: Burton upon Trent.

Begin by heading down to the river ❶ and turn right, later curving right away from the Trent to a T-junction. Turn left to rejoin the riverbank and the path ascends to emerge onto a road. Turn left and at a crossroads turn left again to cross Burton Bridge – over a quarter of a mile wide – enjoying the views up and down the river.

There has been a bridge over the Trent here since the twelfth century. The present structure was opened in 1864 and widened in 1926.

For centuries Burton has been a major centre of the brewing industry. The origins of this lie in the quality of the local water which contains minerals based on the presence of gypsum in the surrounding hills. This was first discovered by monks from the now vanished medieval abbey who obtained the water

Stapenhill Gardens

from wells on the Trent Washlands. During its Victorian heyday around one-quarter of all the beer in the country was brewed in Burton and there were over thirty breweries in the town. Nowadays the number of breweries has vastly declined but the town still remains an important brewing centre and there are several museums to the industry.

The tall brick tower that has dominated the skyline for much of the walk so far is connected with the brewing industry. It is the Bass Tower, a 120-foot (37m) high water tower built in 1866.

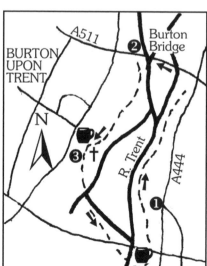

On the other side of the bridge turn left ➋ onto a tarmac track, initially walled. The winding track passes to the left of the Meadowside Leisure Centre, with its adjacent car park, and the library before curving right beside St Modwen's church into the Market Place.

The whole of the area around St Modwen's church and the Market Place occupies the site of the great medieval abbey of Burton, of which there are virtually no surviving remains. The church is Georgian, built around 1720, and the Market Hall was erected in the Victorian era.

At a footpath sign to Memorial Garden and Technical College turn left, passing in front of the Market Hall and Burton College. Go under a bridge, continue between college buildings to a Washlands footpath post and turn left onto Stapenhill Viaduct. ❸ This raised footpath and cycle way takes you above the Washlands and under a road bridge to the Ferry Bridge. Cross it – there are more fine views both up and down the River Trent – to the Boathouse Inn.

River Trent and the Trent Washlands

The Trent Washlands, the flood plain of the river, comprise an attractive mixture of wetlands, meadows and woodlands and provide an unexpected leisure, recreation and wildlife amenity in the heart of the town. The river divides into various channels here, creating islands which can be accessed by bridges. The meadows are still used for grazing and have a surprisingly rural feel. It was the grazing of sheep and the collecting of water from the wells on these rich pastures by the medieval monks that created the two industries, wool and brewing, which became the bases of the prosperity of both the abbey and the town of Burton.

Ferry Bridge replaced an earlier ferry and was opened in 1889. Stapenhill Viaduct was built at the same time and both were donated to the town by Lord Burton.

By the inn turn left into Jerrams Lane and immediately turn left again through Stapenhill Gardens and onto a riverside path. The path passes under St Peter's Bridge and continues by the river to the start.

A Fine Victorian Gothic Church

Jackson's Bank and Hoar Cross

The walk starts and finishes in attractive woodland and the remainder of the route is across fields and along quiet lanes, passing the impressive Victorian church at Hoar Cross. There are fine views over Needwood Forest and the surrounding countryside.

Distance: 4½ miles/7.2km.
Approximate time: 2 hours.
Start: Jackson's Bank (GR SK140233).
Maps: Explorer 245; Landranger 128
Car Parking: Jackson's Bank car park, on side road to Hoar Cross about half a mile (0.8km) west of Newchurch.
Public Transport: None.
Terrain: Woodland tracks and paths at the start and finish, lane and field paths in between, some modest climbs.
Refreshments: None.
Public Toilets: None.

The wooded ridge of Jackson's Bank forms part of the Needwood Estate owned by the Duchy of Lancaster. Much of it was replanted after widespread felling during World War II.

Just north of the car park is a 'Noon Column', one of six designed by the world-renowned artist David Nash. Each of the 3-4m high columns is carved from sustainable English Oak: they are placed so that, at noon each day, the sun shines through a slot carved in the wood, creating a line of light within the shadow cast by the column itself.

Turn left out of the car park ❶ along the road and at a public footpath sign, turn right beside a gate and walk along the right edge of a field. In the field corner, keep ahead along a path through woodland, heading downhill and bending right. At the bottom turn right along a track to a lane.

Turn left, cross a footbridge beside a ford and turn right at a T-junction. At a public footpath sign, turn left ❷ over a stile, walk across a farmyard and bear left between buildings to a stile. Climb it and another one just ahead, continue across a field and climb a stile in the far right corner. Keep across the next field in the direction of the tower of Hoar Cross church, climb a stile in the corner and turn left to walk parallel to the left field edge. At a hedge corner, keep ahead beside the hedge and climb a stile onto a road. Turn right to Hoar Cross church.

This impressive sandstone church was built in the 1870s by Emily Meynell-Ingram, of the adjacent Hoar Cross Hall, as a memorial to her husband who was killed in a hunting accident. It was designed by GF Bodley, one of the foremost architects of the time, and is regarded as one of the finest Victorian Gothic churches in the country.

❸ Opposite the church turn right through a kissing gate and walk across a small wooded area to a stile. From here there is a superb view ahead over the well-wooded land-scape of Needwood

Hoar Cross Church

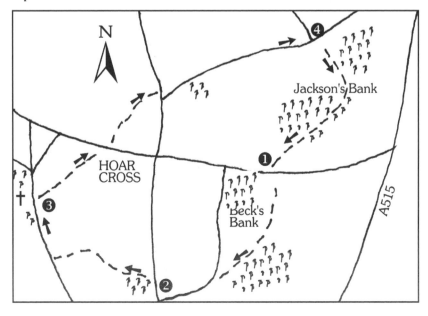

Forest. After climbing the stile, bear slightly left downhill, making for a stile in a dip. Climb it, walk down three steps and turn left along a left field edge. After about 50 yards (46m), bear right across the field and look out for a stile in the fence in front. Climb it, keep ahead by a fence on the left and climb another stile onto a road.

Looking towards Needwood Forest from near Hoar Cross Church

Turn right and at a public footpath sign, turn left over a stile and keep ahead across a field towards a solitary tree. Continue past it to the next tree, bear slightly left to follow the old tree line and in the field corner, turn right over a stile and across a plank footbridge. Walk along the right field edge and climb a stile onto a road.

Turn right and almost immediately turn left along a pleasant, quiet shady lane. After three-quarters of a mile (1.2km) and shortly after passing a lane on the left, turn right through a kissing gate. **4**

Cross a footbridge, walk along the right edge of a field and climb a stile in the corner. Continue along an uphill path through woodland and just before emerging from the trees, turn right – at this point a yellow waymark on a tree trunk indicates that this is part of the 'Branston to Jackson's Bank Walk'.

The path keeps close to the left inside edge of the trees. Bear left on joining another path and this winding and undulating path leads back to the car park.

8

Villages, Woodlands and Canal

Barton-under-Needwood

There is plenty of interest and a series of fine views on this varied walk in Needwood Forest. The first leg is an undulating route across fields, by both new and old woodlands and through two quiet and remote villages. The second half is mostly along the towpath of the Trent and Mersey Canal, passing through Branston Water Park and ending with a walk through a marina on the edge of Barton.

Distance: 8½ miles/13.7km.
Approximate time: 4½ hours.
Start: Barton-under-Needwood, by the war memorial in the village centre (GR SK188185).
Maps: Explorer 245; Landranger 128.
Car Parking: Barton-under-Needwood (free).
Public Transport: Buses from Lichfield and Burton upon Trent.
Terrain: Fields, woodland, a few gentle gradients and a lengthy stretch along a canal towpath.
Refreshments: Pubs at Barton-under-Needwood, pub at Tatenhill, canalside pub on the edge of Branston, pub at Barton Turn.
Public Toilets: Barton-under-Needwood.

There are a number of attractive old buildings and several pubs in Barton-under-Needwood. As its name indicates, the village lies below the wooded slopes of Needwood Forest between the fringes of the old forest and the River Trent. The church was built in the early sixteenth century on the site of an earlier chapel, a rare example of a church built in the Tudor period.

The walk starts in front of the war memorial ❶. Facing the Shoulder of Mutton, turn left, passing to the right of the church, and after almost a quarter of a mile (400m), turn right, at a public bridleway sign, along a track to a gate. Go through, walk along a straight, enclosed track and where the track bends left, keep ahead to go through another gate. Follow a worn path across a field to a footpath post which indicates paths to Dunstall both ahead and to the left.

Take the one to the left and continue across the field to a gate. Go through, here entering the woodland of Smith Hills, a mixture of recent plantings and mature trees, and continue through it, going through two more gates. After leaving the trees, continue in the same direction across a field, passing under electricity pylons and making for a gap in a hedge. To the right is an attractive view of Dunstall church. Go through a gate onto a track, turn right, pass to the left of cottages – there is a pool to the left – go through another gate and keep ahead along a track to emerge

Shoulder of Mutton pub at Barton-under-Needwood

onto a road in front of the church. ❷

The tranquil hamlet of Dunstall comprises little more than the church, hall and a few farms and cottages. The church is Victorian, built in 1853.

Turn right and at a public bridleway sign, turn left gently uphill along a tarmac track. Go through a gate, keep ahead and where the track bends left to a farm, go through another gate and continue along an enclosed grassy track. Climb a stile, keep ahead, go through a gate and continue straight across the next field to a gate on the far side. After going through it, walk along a wide, fence-lined track towards farm buildings, continue between barns and keep ahead along a tarmac track. Follow the track around a right bend but where it bends left, keep ahead through a gate, at a public footpath sign, and continue along an enclosed track. Bend left beside a house, go through a gate and keep ahead to a road.

Turn left and almost immediately turn right along Cuckoo Cage Lane. At a public bridleway sign, turn right along a hedge-lined track, go through a gate and continue along a narrower enclosed path to go through another gate. Continue in the same direction across a field, go through a gate, and keep along the left edge of the next field to a gate in the corner. Go through and continue downhill along a right field edge towards Tatenhill church, later veering left and heading down to go through a gate onto a road. ❸

Like Dunstall, Tatenhill is a small village with a remote feel, though it does boast a pub. The church was once the major church in the area and mostly dates from the thirteenth century. It was restored in the 1890s.

Detour right if you wish to visit the church and – a little further on – the pub, but the route continues to the left through the village. At a public footpath sign, turn right along the bottom right hand edge of a field, follow the edge as it curves left and turn right over a stile. Keep ahead below wooded slopes on the left, cross a path and turn left over a stile to enter Battlestead Hill Wood. The path bends right to head uphill through this beautiful wooded area. Keep ahead at a footpath sign, continue gently downhill and at a fork, take the right hand path down to a stile. From here there is a splendid view over the Trent Valley.

After climbing the stile, continue downhill along the right edge of a field to a gate. Go through and keep ahead along an enclosed path to emerge onto a track. Over to the left the buildings and breweries of Burton upon Trent can be seen. Bear right to the corner of a road, turn left and at a permissive footpath sign and Battlestead and Back waymark, turn right through a gate. Turn left to follow the permissive route along the left edge of two fields, crossing a footbridge between the two and finally emerging onto a track by the Trent and Mersey Canal on the edge of Branston.

Cross the bridge over the canal and turn right down steps by the Bridge Inn to the towpath. ❹ Continue along it and soon you see over to the left and right the pools that make up the Branston Water Park.

The Trent and Mersey Canal was opened in 1777 and linked the River Trent at Shardlow in Derbyshire with the River Mersey at Runcorn in Cheshire, a distance of 93 miles (149km). Branston Water Park, a popular and attractive area of lakes, woodland and wetlands, has been created from a former gravel pit. There is a picnic site and small visitor centre.

Cross a bridge to walk along the right bank of the canal and at the next bridge, cross over again to continue along the left side. Now comes a noisy stretch as the canal runs parallel to the busy A38. Continue under a succession of bridges as far as Bridge 38 where you bear left off the towpath and turn right to cross the bridge. **❺** Walk along the road and turn left into Barton Turns Marina.

Turn right through the car park, take the well-surfaced path along the left side of the pool and at a fork, continue along the left hand path which curves right in front of another pool. Do not continue along this path but take the parallel grassy path, by a ditch on the right. Later keep along an enclosed path which emerges into a sports field.

Immediately turn right over a footbridge and stile, bear left across a field, gradually curving left, and cross another footbridge and stile in the left hand corner. Head across the grass to climb a stile and walk along a tarmac track beside a tree-fringed pool on the left to a road. Turn right into Barton and at a T-junction turn left along Main Street to the start.

Trent & Mersey Canal near Branston Water Park

A Waterside Ramble

Fradley Junction and Alrewas

The first leg is an invigorating stroll along the towpath of the Trent and Mersey Canal, with fine views in all directions, to the village of Alrewas. This is followed by a walk across riverside meadows with a very attractive stretch beside the Trent. Enclosed tracks, field paths and a short section beside the A513 bring you to a lane which returns you to the start.

Distance: 7½ miles/12.1km.
Approximate time: 3½ hours.
Start: Fradley Junction, by the café and information centre, signposted from A513 to the south west of Alrewas (GR SK142141).
Maps: Explorer 245; Landranger 128.
Car Parking: Pay car park at Fradley Junction.
Public Transport: None but you could start the walk at Alrewas which is served by buses from Birmingham, Lichfield and Burton upon Trent.
Terrain: Flat and easy walking on a canal towpath, across riverside meadows, on field paths and along a lane; mud likely in places.
Refreshments: Pub and café at Fradley Junction, pubs at Alrewas.
Public Toilets: At start.

T he canalside cottages and pub at Fradley Junction, the meeting place of the Coventry and Trent and Mersey canals, make an attractive scene. The Trent and Mersey Canal was opened in 1777 and linked the River Trent at Shardlow in Derbyshire with the River Mersey at Runcorn in Cheshire, a distance of 93 miles (149km). The Coventry Canal, which runs between here and Coventry, was completed in 1790. The original wharf buildings have been converted into a café, shop and information centre.

Facing the canal ❶ turn right alongside it, turn left over the first bridge and immediately turn right to continue along the other bank. Follow the towpath for just over 1½ miles (2.4km) into Alrewas and in front of bridge 48, leave the canal and head up to the road. Cross over and continue along Mill End Lane, passing to the left of the church.

Trent & Mersey Canal between Fradley Junction and Alrewas

The pleasant village of Alrewas gets its name from a combination of alder and marsh. Alder trees like damp conditions and thrived in the marshy, low-lying ground by the Trent. It has a number of attractive old buildings, including some half-timbered, thatched cottages. The impressive sandstone church dates mainly from the thirteenth and fourteenth centuries but retains an earlier Norman doorway at the base of the tower.

Keep ahead at a junction – still along Mill End Lane – and where the lane

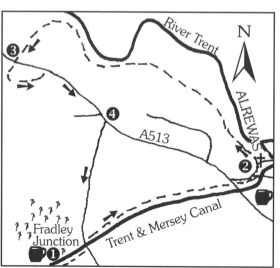

ends, turn left, at a public footpath sign, along an enclosed path to a stile. ❷ Climb it and turn right to follow a worn path across a field. In the corner pass between redundant gateposts, keep initially along the left edge of the next field but before reaching the corner, bear right across it to a stile.

After climbing it, keep ahead across the next three fields, passing through a series of hedge gaps, but in the fourth field bear slightly left across it to a stile. Climb it onto a track, turn right and at a waymarked post, turn left onto another track. At the next waymarked post, bear slightly right across a field to climb a stile on the far side and continue along the right edge of the next field. At the corner of the hedge on the right, bear left to head across to the left edge of the field and keep along it to a stile in the corner.

River Trent near Alrewas

Climb the stile and walk along a track beside the River Trent. Where the track bends left, keep ahead over a stile and continue beside the river to a gate in the corner of the meadow. Go through, keep ahead, cross a footbridge and now leave the river by curving left across the next meadow and making for a hedge corner. Continue along the left edge of the meadow to a waymark, go through a gap, walk along the right edge of a field and climb a stile onto a track.

Turn left and follow the enclosed track to the A513. ❸ Turn right and almost immediately left along another enclosed track. Climb a stile, keep ahead and on reaching a brook, turn left through a fence gap. Walk beside the brook along the right edge of a field, keep along the right edge of the next field and look out for where a yellow waymark directs you to turn left and continue across the field to the far side. Here you have to negotiate some rough ground in order to emerge onto the A513 again at a public footpath sign.

Turn right and now comes an unavoidable stretch of walking along the main road but it is only for about half a mile (800m) and there is a wide verge all the way. Turn right along the lane signposted to Fradley Junction ❹ and follow it for a mile (1.6km) to the Trent and Mersey Canal. After crossing the canal bridge, turn right to return to the start.

10

A Poignant Tribute

National Memorial Arboretum, Alrewas and Wychnor

From the sylvan surroundings of the National Memorial Arboretum the route takes you through the attractive village of Alrewas to the Trent and Mersey Canal. The canal towpath is followed to picturesque Wychnor church and on to Wychnor Lock. After a noisy but mercifully brief stretch alongside the busy A38, the walk continues across pleasant and peaceful riverside meadows to Alrewas and back to the start.

Distance: 5½ miles/8.9km *plus any walking around the Arboretum.*
Approximate time: 2½ hours.
Start: National Memorial Arboretum, just off the A513 about three-quarters of a mile (1.2km) to the east of Alrewas, signposted from A513 and A38 (GR SK181146).
Maps: Explorer 245; Landranger 128.
Car Parking: Free parking at the National Memorial Arboretum.
Public Transport: Nothing direct, but you could start the walk from Alrewas which is served by buses from Birmingham, Lichfield and Burton upon Trent.
Terrain: Some road walking but mostly canal towpath and riverside meadows.
Refreshments: Café at the National Memorial Arboretum Visitor Centre, pubs at Alrewas.
Public Toilets: National Memorial Arboretum.

Conceived as a result of a visit to Washington in 1988, the National Memorial Arboretum is a most poignant and thought provoking place. It is managed by the Royal British Legion as a permanent monument to all who have suffered or died in the service of their country, not just in war but in their jobs or through acts of terrorism. Planting began in 1997 on land previously used for gravel extraction alongside the River Tame with funding provided by The National Forest Company. So far 40,000 trees have been planted but the project is evolving all the while and there is still much to do. There is a visitor centre with a shop and restaurant. Parking is free but you are invited to make a donation.

Begin by retuning to the road ❶, turn left and follow it around a right bend to the A513. Cross over, continue along the road ahead (Barley Green

One of the memorials in the National Memorial Arboretum

Lane) and take the first lane on the right. This soon becomes a rough track called Ridget Lane. Climb a metal ladder stile over a conveyor belt – extraction is still taking place in the vicinity – turn right alongside it and climb steps up to the A513.

Turn left, cross a railway bridge, keep ahead at a road junction, in the Kings Bromley and Rugeley direction, and cross the A38. Continue along the road and after a quarter of a mile (400m), turn right along Fox Lane to a crossroads in the village centre of Alrewas. At the crossroads keep ahead along Post Office Road to a T-junction, turn left to cross a canal bridge and immediately turn right onto the towpath of the Trent and Mersey Canal. ❷

The pleasant village of Alrewas gets its name from a combination of alder and marsh. Alder trees like damp conditions and thrived in the marshy, low-lying ground by the Trent. It has a number of attractive old buildings, including some half-timbered, thatched cottages. The impressive sandstone church dates

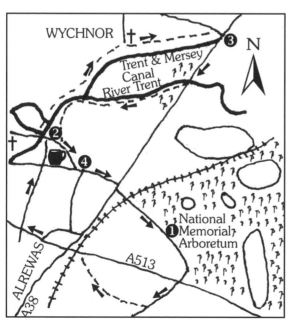

Approaching Wychnor Church along the towpath of the Trent & Mersey Canal

mainly from the thirteenth and fourteenth centuries but retains an earlier Nor-man doorway at the base of the tower.

The Trent and Mersey Canal was opened in 1777 and linked the River Trent at Shardlow in Derbyshire with the River Mersey at Runcorn in Cheshire, a distance of 93 miles (149km). Just beyond Alrewas the river and canal briefly merge.

As you walk beside the canal a grand view opens up ahead of the tower of Wychnor church and you cross bridges over two arms of the River Trent where the river and canal merge. A little further on they separate again and the route continues by the canal. Just before a bridge a brief detour to the left over a stile, up across a field and through a kissing gate brings you to Wychnor church.

The medieval church at Wychnor has a delightful location just above the canal and overlooking the Trent Valley. The village it once served became deserted and has all but disappeared. Its site is in the fields on the opposite side of the lane.

Return to the canal and continue along it to Wychnor Lock. **❸** Here turn right over a bridge to the A38 and turn right along it. This is an unavoidably noisy stretch of the walk but fortunately you only have to walk along the road for just over a quarter of a mile (400m). There is a footpath and it is worth it in order to gain access to the riverbank.

At a public footpath sign immediately after crossing a bridge over the River Trent, turn right down an embankment, climb a stile and walk beside the river. After climbing the next stile, continue along the edge of Essington Meadows, a new plantation financed through The National Forest, and climb another stile at the far end. There are superb views to the right across the river to Wychnor church. Keep across the riverside meadows, later continuing by the canal, and on approaching Alrewas, bear left across the meadow away from the canal and go through a kissing gate in the corner. Walk along a path and then a tarmac track to a road and turn left into Alrewas.

Turn right along King William Road and at a T-junction, turn left **4** and the road emerges onto the A38. Cross very carefully – heeding the signs – turn right and almost immediately turn left. The road leads back to the entrance to the National Memorial Arboretum.

The tower of Wychnor Church from the banks of the River Trent

11

A Forestry Transformation

Rosliston and Walton-on-Trent

An initial stroll through conifer woodland is followed by an easy walk across fields to the village of Walton-on-Trent. On the return leg some gentle climbing and more field walking brings you to Rosliston and a final short wooded stretch leads back to the start.

Distance: 5 miles/8km.
Approximate time: 2½ hours.
Start: Rosliston Forestry Centre, half a mile (800m) north of Rosliston village, (GR SK244175).
Maps: Explorer 245; Landranger 128.
Car Parking: Pay car park at Rosliston Forestry Centre.
Public Transport: Infrequent bus service from Swadlincote and Burton upon Trent.
Terrain: Forest tracks, quiet roads and field paths.
Refreshments: Café at Forestry Centre, pubs at Walton-on-Trent, pub at Rosliston.
Public Toilets: At the start.

Rosliston Forestry Centre is one of the flagship sites of The National Forest. Since 1993 grants from the National Forest Company, the Forestry Commission and South Derbyshire District Council have helped to transform a former farm just to the north of Rosliston village into this attractive recreational area whose wide ranging facilities include a visitor centre, shop, educational facilities and restaurant. There are walking trails, cycle tracks, a children's play area, lakes, meadows and a mixture of old and more recent woodlands.

From the Centre **1** walk back to the road, turn right and at a public footpath sign to Drakelow, turn left over a stile. Do not follow the direction of the footpath sign but turn sharp left onto a grassy path which runs parallel to the road for a few yards before bending right. Immediately turn left over a stile and turn right onto a path through trees and by a hedge on the right. Follow the path around a left bend and climb a stile onto a road.

Turn right along this winding road and after about three-quarters of a mile (1.2km) where the road bends sharply left, turn right onto the track to Fairfield Farm **2** and immediately turn left along the left edge of a field. After going

Plantation near Rosliston

through a gate, continue along the right edge of a succession of fields and over a series of stiles, eventually emerging onto a tarmac track which leads to a road on the edge of Walton-on-Trent. Keep ahead to a T-junction, turn left along Main Street and opposite the White Swan, turn right along Station Road, passing the church, to Walton Bridge.

The church at Walton-on-Trent is of Norman origins with a fine fifteenth century west tower. For centuries this has been an important crossing point

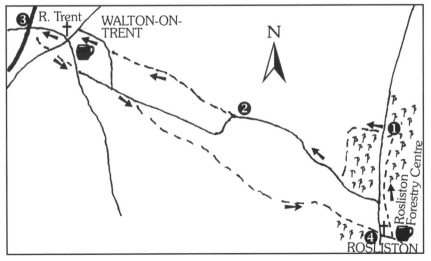

over the River Trent but the first bridge was not built until 1834, replaced twice since then. Borough Hill to the south of the village was probably the site of an Iron Age fort.

Just before the bridge, turn left along an enclosed path **❸** and on emerging onto the end of a road, keep along it to a T-junction. Turn left back into the village and at a public footpath sign, turn right onto another enclosed path. Go through a kissing gate, keep ahead and the path becomes a tarmac drive which leads to a road junction. Cross Coton Road, take the road ahead and just after the last of the houses, turn right over a stile.

Bear left and head diagonally uphill across a field, looking out for a stile in the fence ahead just to the right of a belt of trees. Climb it, maintain the same direction across the next field and climb a stile in the far right hand corner. Follow a faint path across a field, climb a stile and walk along the right edge of the next two fields. In the second field, turn right at a hedge corner to continue along the right field edge, follow the edge to the left and after going through the next hedge gap, immediately turn right over a footbridge. Continue along the right edge of the next field to a stile, climb it and turn left along a left field edge.

After passing through a gap, bear right diagonally across a field, climb a stile and continue in the same direction across the next field. Cross a footbridge, bear right diagonally across a field and climb a waymarked stile in the corner. Walk along an enclosed path which emerges into a field and keep along its right edge towards the houses of Rosliston. In the corner turn right over a footbridge, turn left along an enclosed path, climb a stile and keep ahead to a road in Rosliston. **❹**

The small church at Rosliston was rebuilt in the early nineteenth century and the fourteenth century west tower is all that remains of its medieval predecessor.

Turn right, follow the road around a left bend and after about 100 yards (91m), turn left along a track between cottages and houses – the church is to the left – to a public footpath sign to Rosliston Farm. Walk along an enclosed path to enter a field and bear slightly left across it to a gate on the far side. Go through and at a T-junction in front, turn left onto a path through trees which leads back to the car park.

12

Fields and Woodlands

Coton in the Elms

The walk explores some of the new woodlands to the east of the village of Coton in the Elms planted through The National Forest scheme. It reveals clearly how rapidly parts of the landscape are changing as a result of that scheme. From several points there are extensive views across the Mease and Trent valleys.

Distance: 4 miles/6.4km.
Approximate time: 2 hours.
Start: Coton Wood, a quarter of a mile (400m) south of Coton in the Elms (GR SK245148).
Maps: Explorer 245; Landranger 128.
Car Parking: Small free car park at Coton Wood.
Public Transport: Buses from Swadlincote and Burton upon Trent.
Terrain: Easy walking with gentle gradients across fields and through recent plantations.
Refreshments: Pubs at Coton in the Elms.
Public Toilets: None.

With your back to the road **1**, pass beside the fence at the far end of the car park into the wood – there is an information board here – and walk along a path to a crossways.

By the standards of many of the woods in The National Forest, Coton Wood is relatively mature woodland. It was planted by the Woodland Trust in 1994 on what was formerly farmland and comprises mainly native broadleaved trees, including oak, ash, cherry and hawthorn.

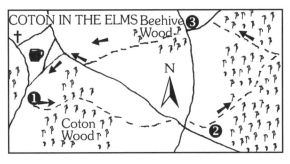

Turn left, then left again and the path curves right. Take the first path on the left, turn left again at a T-junction and when you see a waymarked stile on the left, turn half-right. Continue through the trees, keep ahead at a crossways and climb a stile and cross a footbridge on the edge of the wood.

Walk along the right edge of a field and at the corner of the hedge on the right, continue straight ahead and climb a stile on the far side. Cross a track, climb the stile opposite, continue across two more fields and climb a stile onto a road. Keep ahead and at a crossroads, pass beside a fence barrier and continue in the same direction along the right edge of Sisters Wood parallel to the road. At another fence barrier and metal gate on the right, ❷ turn left and head in a straight line along a broad green track through the plantation towards woodland. Go through a hedge gap, keep ahead, bear left on joining another path and go through another hedge gap into Top Wood.

Continue gently uphill along the right field edge to a stile, climb it and bear right to climb another one. Keep along the right edge of the next field, over a series of stiles, and on joining a track by farm buildings, turn sharp left onto it. Follow the track alongside the plantation of Top Wood on the right down to a road. Turn left to a T-junction, turn right and immediately turn left, at a public footpath sign, along a tarmac drive. ❸

Keep in a straight line through another plantation (Beehive Wood), continue through a thicket but before reaching the end of it, turn left and walk between a hedge on the right and a small pool on the left. Keep in a straight line, passing a waymarked post, head across the corner of a field and go through a very wide gap in a hedge. Continue diagonally across a large field, making for the far right corner where you emerge onto a road in front of a white house. Turn right into Coton in the Elms and by the Queens Head, turn left along Mill Street, passing along the left edge of a triangular green.

The elm trees that gave the former farming and mining village of Coton in the Elms its name have long since gone, the victims of Dutch elm disease. It is an attractive village with a triangular green watered by a stream and frequented by ducks. The Victorian Gothic church was built in 1846.

Keep ahead for a quarter of a mile (400m) to return to the car park.

13

The Forest's Industrial Heritage

Moira Furnace and the Ashby Canal

This walk is in the heart of The National Forest and vividly illustrates the changes that have taken place recently in the landscape of what was once a busy, noisy and unattractive mining area. Coal tips and colliery buildings have been replaced by woodland, small lakes, nature reserves and picnic sites but the industrial heritage is preserved through the canal and fascinating group of buildings around Moira Furnace. The walk utilises two means of transport once used to carry coal: the Ashby Canal and a disused railway track, the latter now the Ashby Woulds Heritage Trail.

Distance: 3½ miles/5.6km.
Approximate time: 2 hours.
Start: Moira Furnace, just off B5003 to west of Moira village (GR SK314153).
Maps: Explorer 245; Landranger 128.
Car Parking: Free car park at Moira Furnace.
Public Transport: Buses from Coalville, Ashby-de-la-Zouch and Swadlincote.
Terrain: Easy flat walking on tracks, field paths and a canal towpath with one stretch along a road.
Refreshments: Tea room at Moira Furnace, pub at Donisthorpe.
Public Toilets: At start.

Moira gets its name from the Earls of Moira who owned much of the land in the locality and it was the second earl who began the development of many of the coal mines around the village in the early nineteenth century. He also built the blast furnace beside the recently completed Ashby Canal in 1806 in order to process iron ore extracted from the coal deposits. It was never successful, mainly because of insufficient quantities of ore and considerable variation in its quality, and the furnace was closed the following year. An attempt was made to start it up again in 1810 but after only nine months it closed down for good.

Moira Furnace and the adjacent limekilns have been restored and opened to the public as a museum, with displays and information boards explaining how the furnace worked. The site also has craft workshops and a small nature reserve.

Facing the children's' play area **❶**, turn left across the car park and continue across a sports field, making for the far left hand corner. Cross the end of a tarmac track and continue along the path opposite which curves left into woodland to a kissing gate. Go through and just before reaching the next gate, turn right up a flight of steps to the top of a railway embankment and at the top turn left onto a path.

The path is part of the Ashby Woulds Heritage Trail between Moira and Measham which runs along the

Moira Furnace

former track of the Ashby and Nuneaton Joint Railway. The railway was opened in 1873 to carry coal from the local mines to London and the south of England. It finally closed in 1981.

The path soon passes through Donisthorpe Woodland Park.

The woodland park has been established on the site of the former Donisthorpe Colliery. Soon after its closure in 1990, the site was acquired from British coal and most of the planting was carried out in 1996-97. Funding was provided by The National Forest Company and it is a superb example of how a former industrial area can be made attractive again and provide

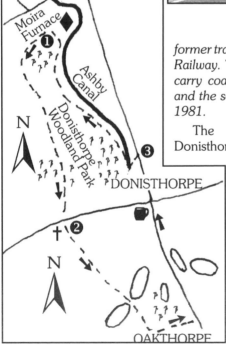

recreational facilities. A series of information boards illustrate the immense task involved in achieving this transformation in a relatively short time.

Follow the path, winding in places, over a stream and it eventually emerges onto a road. Cross over, turn right and the path curves left into a parking area by Donisthorpe's early nineteenth century church. Turn left to continue along the disused railway track but at a fork take the left hand path, ❷ here leaving the Heritage Trail.

Go through a fence gap and the enclosed path continues along the backs of houses to a stile. Climb it, walk along the right edge of a field and keep ahead through a belt of trees. After crossing a footbridge, there follows a most attractive part of the route as you continue between pools, over marshy land and then along a left field edge, with views of the village of Oakthorpe in front. An enclosed section rises gently to reach the end of a lane. Turn left along a track, at a public footpath sign, and climb a stile onto a road.

Turn left along the road for half a mile (800m) – there are attractive stretches of water on both sides – to a crossroads in Donisthorpe. Keep ahead along Moira Road and just beyond the last of the houses on the left, turn left into the Donisthorpe Woodland car park. ❸ Head up to go through a gate to the Ashby Canal, turn left and then right across the end of the canal and turn right again along the towpath.

The Ashby Canal was built between 1794 and 1804 and linked the coal mines around Moira with the Coventry Canal at Marston Junction near Nuneaton. It declined after it was largely superseded by the railway and this, coupled with instability caused by mining subsidence, led to its closure in the 1940s. The short stretch from here to Conkers Discovery Centre has been restored and there are plans to open up more. The southerly, more agricultural section of the canal from Snarestone is still in use and is a popular recreational amenity.

Follow the canal to Moira Furnace and in front of the bridge, turn left downhill beside the furnace. Keep ahead along a tarmac drive and take the first turning on the left to return to the car park.

14

Ivanhoe's Castle

Ashby-de-la-Zouch, Blackfordby and Smisby

The walk takes you across the gently rolling countryside to the west, north and east of Ashby-de-la-Zouch. Initially a straight path leads across fields to the hilltop village of Blackfordby. From there you head across to Smisby and a gentle descent brings you back to Ashby town centre. There are a number of fine and extensive views and the route passes by several recently planted woods created through The National Forest project.

Distance: 7 miles/11.3km.
Approximate time: 3½ hours.
Start: Ashby-de-la-Zouch, in Market Street in front of the Town Hall and Market building (GR SK358167).
Maps: Explorer 245; Landranger 128.
Car Parking: Pay car parks in the centre of Ashby.
Public Transport: Buses from Leicester, Nuneaton, Burton upon Trent, Swadlincote, Coalville, Nottingham, Tamworth, Birmingham and surrounding villages.
Terrain: Mainly field and woodland paths and tracks with a few gentle gradients.
Refreshments: Pubs and cafés at Ashby, pub at Blackfordby, pub at Smisby.
Public Toilets: Ashby.

Although situated in the former Leicestershire coalfield with industrial towns and mining villages nearby, Ashby-de-la-Zouch never became industrialised itself and retains the atmosphere of a pleasant and traditional old market town. It gets its name from the Zouches who became lords of the manor in 1160 and added their family name to distinguish the town from other Ashbys in the Midlands.

In the fifteenth century the manor passed to the powerful Hastings family and Sir William Hastings was given royal permission to transform the fortified manor house into a strong castle. He mainly did this by constructing the impressive Hastings Tower, around 90 feet (27m) high and comprising four storeys. As a Royalist stronghold in the Civil War, Ashby Castle had to endure a lengthy siege by Parliamentary forces during which the Hastings Tower was split in two. After the war the castle was slighted on the orders of Cromwell's government but in the nineteenth century Sir Walter Scott caused a renewal of interest in it by making it the setting for his Ivanhoe stories.

The nearby church was built in the fifteenth century and restored and enlarged in 1880. Inside there are monuments to the Hastings family.

Hastings Tower at Ashby Castle

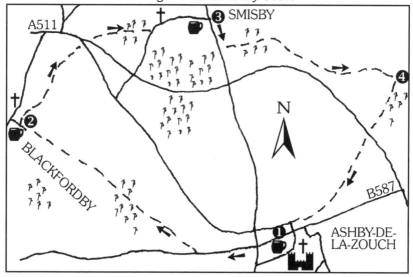

Facing the Town Hall and Market ❶, turn right along Market Street and at a junction keep ahead uphill along Kilwardby Street. The street continues as Moira Road and soon after going over the brow of the hill, you turn right into Highfields Close. Turn left at a T-junction and where the road ends, turn right onto an enclosed tarmac path.

The path bears left along the right edge of a sports field to a road. Cross over and the well-waymarked route continues in a more or less straight line across a series of fields, over stiles and through hedge gaps, heading gently uphill towards Blackfordby. Finally you climb a stile onto a lane which leads into the village.

The tiny village of Blackfordby retains a few old thatched cottages. The church was originally a chapel which had fallen into disrepair by the Victorian era and was rebuilt in the 1850s.

Keep ahead to a T-junction in order to visit the pub and church but just before reaching there, the route continues to the right along an enclosed track. ❷ The track curves right between trees to a gate. Go through, bear left along the left field edge and in the corner, bear slightly right to continue along the left edge of the next field to a waymarked post. Turn left through a fence gap, head across the field, go through another gap and continue across the next field, making for a stile near the far right corner.

After climbing it, cross a road and take the narrow enclosed path ahead. Climb another stile, keep ahead to cross the A511, descend an embankment on the other side and go through a kissing gate. Walk across to a stile, climb it, keep ahead to climb another one and continue to a field corner where you cross a plank footbridge and climb a stile into the next field. Continue across it, climb a stile on the far side and walk along a track between recent National Forest woodlands to a kissing gate. Go through and keep along a lane into the village of Smisby.

Smisby is a traditional farming village just across the Leicestershire-Derbyshire border. The fine church is mainly fourteenth century with a fifteenth century tower. It was restored in the late nineteenth century.

After passing the church, the lane bears slightly right and continues through the village to a T-junction. ❸ Turn right and after a quarter of a mile (400m), turn left along a lane – there is a sign here Public Bridleway 150 yards ahead – passing between The National Forest woodlands of Woodcote. The lane becomes more of a tarmac drive and where it curves left to a farm, turn right beside a barrier and walk along a track by a wire fence on the left.

The track bears left and for a while keeps parallel to the A511. From here there are extensive views to both right and left. Follow the track to the gates of a farm and turn right ❹ along the left edge of a field to emerge onto a tarmac drive. Continue along it and at a junction of tracks and paths (just before the drive curves left), turn right along a hedge-lined track, here joining the

Smisby Church

well-waymarked Ivanhoe Way. At a fork take the right hand track – now attractively tree-lined – pass under the A511 and keep ahead, passing by the huge McVitie's building, largely screened from the path by trees.

Where the track bears slightly left, turn right over a plank footbridge and walk along an enclosed path. Look out for where you turn right over another footbridge, turn left and the path bends right to enter a field. Turn left, follow the path across the field towards the corner of houses and continue on to a kissing gate in the far right corner. Go through, continue across the next field, go through a hedge gap and walk along the left field edge to go through another kissing gate.

Take the enclosed path opposite which continues along a left field edge. It becomes enclosed again and finally a tarmac track brings you onto a road. Turn left and at a T-junction, turn right and continue down Market Street to return to the start.

15

Hall, Church and Parkland

Staunton Harold

Most of the first half of the walk is across part of the well-wooded Staunton Harold Estate, giving you the opportunity to see the unforgettable and highly photogenic combination of hall, church and lake situated amidst rolling parkland. The return leg is across fields with some fine and extensive views.

Distance: 5½ miles/8.9km.
Approximate time: 3 hours.
Start: Car park at the southern end of Staunton Harold Reservoir (GR SK378220).
Maps: Explorer 245; Landranger 128.
Car Parking: Severn Trent Water car park (free) at southern end of Staunton Harold Reservoir. Take lane signposted to Calke from B587.
Public Transport: None.
Terrain: Woodland, parkland and field walking, gentle terrain.
Refreshments: Tea room at Ferrers Craft Centre at Staunton Harold Hall.
Public Toilets: None.

From the car park ❶ take the path that heads down to the lane. Bend right to cross the end of the reservoir and shortly turn left to enter the Dimminsdale Nature Reserve. *Just south of the car park can be seen one of the six 'Noon Columns' (see p. 34).*

Staunton Harold Reservoir was constructed in 1964 and extends over an area of 209 acres. It has become an important wildlife habitat and a popular centre for water sports, fishing, bird watching, cycling and walking.

The nature reserve has been created from a former limestone quarrying area worked since the Middle Ages and the numerous small pools were formed when the disused quarries filled up with water. In February it is noted for its superb display of snowdrops.

Follow a winding path through the wooded reserve and after descending steps to a T-junction, turn right onto a path which later bends sharply left to cross a footbridge over a stream. Climb steps and at a public footpath sign for the Ivanhoe Way, turn right through a squeezer stile. Keep along a path which after the next stile leaves the woodland to continue along the left edge of a field. Where the edge bends left, keep ahead, following the regular waymarks, to emerge onto a lane.

Turn right to a road junction, turn left and at an Ivanhoe Way sign about 100 yards (91m) ahead, turn left again along a tarmac drive. **❷** Look out for a public footpath sign where you turn left over a stile – here leaving the Ivanhoe Way – and walk along the right edge of a field to a kissing gate. Go through, keep along the right edge of the next field and just before the corner, turn right through another kissing gate and turn left along a left field edge towards woodland.

After climbing a stile, keep along the right edge of three fields, climbing a succession of stiles, and then head diagonally across the next field to a waymarked post where you join a tarmac drive by Staunton Harold Hall. Turn right and in front of a No Through road sign, turn left **❸** along the edge of a car park, cross

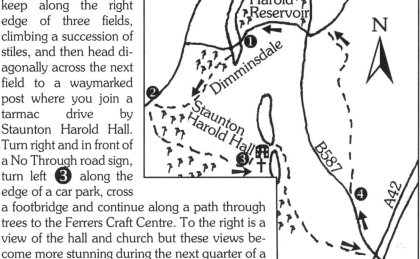

a footbridge and continue along a path through trees to the Ferrers Craft Centre. To the right is a view of the hall and church but these views become more stunning during the next quarter of a mile (400m). Keep ahead on joining a tarmac drive which curves right to a T-junction. Turn right to visit the church; otherwise turn left and cross a bridge over the lake.

The scene of the hall and church at Staunton Harold in close proximity, standing above the lake and surrounded by parkland, could hardly be more typically English. It is all the work of one family, the Shirleys, who owned the estate from 1423 to 1954. Despite this both the hall and family have had a very chequered history.

One member was sent to the Tower of London in the Cromwellian period but later in the seventeenth century the family fortunes revived and the title Earl Ferrers was given to the Shirleys by Queen Anne in 1711. In 1760 the fourth earl was hanged for killing his steward and the family was plagued by debts during the late nineteenth and early twentieth centuries. In 1954 these debts led to the sale of the estate and the hall became first a Cheshire Home and later a Sue Ryder Home. Since 2003 it has been owned by John Blunt.

Staunton Harold Church and Hall from across the lake

The present hall, a restrained and dignified Classical design, was built in the eighteenth century and the formal gardens were laid out at the same time.

The church was built by Sir Robert Shirley in 1653, a rare example of a church dating from the Cromwell era. Built in the traditional Gothic style, this bold Anglican gesture was really a sign of defiance to Oliver Cromwell and the Puritans, hence Sir Robert's incarceration in the Tower of London. It was given to the National Trust prior to the sale of the estate in the 1950s.

Continue through the ornamental gates and take the first track on the right. Go through a kissing gate beside a cattle grid, pass beside a gate and turn right along a tarmac drive. Where the drive bends right, turn left through a gate along a gently ascending track.

At a junction by a waymarked post, keep ahead and the track eventually bends left to a drive. Turn right to a road, turn left in Reservoir and Calke Abbey direction and after half a mile (800m) you reach a public footpath sign on the right. ❹ A lay-by on the opposite side of the road gives a fine view of the hall, church and lake nestling in the valley below.

At the public footpath sign turn right through a hedge gap and head in a straight line across a field. From here there is a view of the hilltop church at Breedon, a prominent landmark for miles around. Climb a stile on the far side, keep ahead to climb another one and walk along the right edge of a field to climb a stile onto a track. Walk along the right edge of the next field, turn right over a footbridge, climb a stile and continue along a left field edge. Go through a hedge gap, keep along the left edge of the next field but after a few yards, turn left over a double stile, here rejoining the Ivanhoe Way.

Head across a field to a waymarked post on the far side, climb two stiles in quick succession, continue across the next field and on by the left field edge to a stile. Climb it onto a lane and turn left to a T-junction. Turn left in the Ashby direction and take the first lane on the right, signposted to Calke, to return to the car park.

16

Medieval Ruins

Cademan Wood, Osgathorpe and Grace Dieu Priory

This walk in Charnwood Forest is lengthy and fairly demanding but well worth the effort. The first and last sections are through the hilltop Cademan Wood. The middle stretch is an undulating route across fields and farmland between Whitwick and Osgathorpe, followed by a walk along a quiet lane to the atmospheric remains of Grace Dieu Priory. More fine woodland near the priory is enjoyed before the return to Cademan Wood. The many fine views and the quiet and seemingly unspoilt countryside disguise the fact that this was once an industrial area. You do need to heed the directions carefully as the route is quite complex with lots of changes of direction and a multitude of gates and stiles.

Distance: 8 miles/12.9km.
Approximate time: 4½ hours.
Start: Cademan Wood, small car park on Swannymote Road between Whitwick and Shepshed (GR SK444168).
Maps: Explorer 245; Landranger 129.
Car Parking: Free car park at Cademan Wood.
Public Transport: None.
Terrain: Mixture of woodland and open fields, a few hilly stretches and 26 stiles to climb.
Refreshments: Pubs at Whitwick, pub at Osgathorpe, pub at Thringstone (brief detour).
Public Toilets: None.

C ademan Wood, a surviving remnant of Charnwood Forest, occupies a plateau which rises to a height of 646 feet (197m). Together with neighbouring woods, it makes up some of the finest and most beautiful areas of broadleaved woodlands in Leicestershire today. The wood is dotted with granite outcrops and from its fringes there are fine views in all directions.

Begin by turning left out of the car park **1** along the road and at a public footpath sign to Thringstone, turn left through a fence gap into Cademan Wood, here joining the Ivanhoe Way. The path initially keeps along the right inside edge of the trees and later continues through the wood. There are a number of paths through the wood and you need to keep a sharp look out for the regular waymarks. However at one point where there is a fork, take the right hand path even though – at the time of writing – a waymark incorrectly indicates the left hand path.

Eventually you emerge into a small grassy area. Keep across it, briefly re-enter the trees and on emerging into a larger area of open grassland, keep along its right edge. If you happen to take the wrong path and reach this open area at a different point, simply make your way across to the right edge to pick up the correct path. Head downhill, curving right to a waymarked post. Bear left, continue downhill along an enclosed path to a road ❷ and turn left

Cademan Wood

downhill into Whitwick.

Whitwick once had a Norman castle but of this there is no trace. With the development of the Leicestershire coalfield, a colliery was opened here in 1826. This finally closed in 1986 and the only visible evidence of Whitwick's history as a mining village is the former colliery headstocks seen later on the walk. In 1898 there was a terrible disaster at the mine when fire broke out, killing 35 miners.

Keep ahead on joining a main road and head uphill to a crossroads. Take the road opposite (Brooks Lane) but almost immediately turn right into School Lane. Where the road ends, keep ahead along an enclosed path, go through a gate and head downhill along the right edge of a field. Cross a footbridge at the bottom, continue uphill along the right field edge, climb a stile at the top and keep along the right edge of the next two fields, bearing left away from the edge in the second field and making for a waymarked stile. Climb it, cross a lane and climb the stile opposite. Bear slightly left downhill across the next field and climb another stile at the bottom. It is on this descent that the headstocks of the former Whitwick Colliery can be seen.

Keep ahead across the next field, pass through a narrow belt of trees and turn left along the left field edge. Go through another belt of trees, cross a footbridge over a stream, keep ahead across a field and climb a stile on the far side. Turn right through an area of scattered trees, turn left to make for a waymarked post and turn right to pass behind buildings to a stile. Climb it, walk along an enclosed path, climbing two more stiles, and finally head across to climb another stile onto a lane. **❸**

Cross over, climb the stile opposite and at a public footpath sign to Griffydam, turn right along the right edge of a field, veering left away from it to climb a stile. Keep ahead across the next field, go through a small group of trees, continue along an enclosed path and climb a stile onto a road. Climb the stile opposite, walk along the right field edge, climb another stile in the corner and continue along the left edge of the next two fields. In the corner of the second field curve left to climb a stile onto the A512.

Turn right for a few yards and at a public footpath sign, turn left through a gap and go up steps to climb a stile. Walk across the field to a waymarked post and continue along the right field edge. Pass through two hedge gaps, keep along the right edge of the next field and climb a stile beside a gate. Turn left along the left edge of a field, climb a stile and bear right across the next field – here leaving the Ivanhoe Way – making for the corner of a hedge. Continue by a hedge on the left to a stile in the field corner, climb it, walk along the left edge of a field and in the corner turn right to continue along the field edge to a gate.

Go through, walk along the left field edge, turn left over a stile in the corner and keep straight ahead across the next field to climb a stile onto a lane. **❹** Turn right uphill and at a public footpath sign, turn left through a hedge gap and walk across a field, keeping to the right of a telegraph pole, to a waymarked post on the far side. Turn right along the left field edge, at the next waymarked post, turn left along a fence-lined path to enter a field and continue along its right edge. Go through a gap in the field corner and head straight across the next field, making for a waymarked post on the far side where you go through a hedge gap.

Turn right along the right field edge, follow the edge around left and right bends and continue along an enclosed path. The path bends left in front of a cottage, then turns right and becomes a track which emerges onto a road in Osgathorpe.

Osgathorpe is an obvious Viking place name, an indication that this area of England was during part of the ninth and tenth centuries under the rule of Danish Vikings. Despite being near the A512 and quite close to the towns of Coalville and Ashby-de-la-Zouch, the village has a genuinely remote feel. The modest church dates mainly from the fourteenth century, extended and restored in the 1860s.

Keep ahead through the village to a T-junction and turn right along a lane which heads gently downhill to the A512 in front of the remains of Grace Dieu Priory. ❺ Cross the road and turn right along a tarmac path to follow the Grace Dieu Trail, part of Cycle Route 52. Curve left to go through a gate and continue along the winding path, with views of the ruins on the left, to a gate.

The ruins of Grace Dieu Priory

While visiting the local area, William Wordsworth wrote of the 'ivied ruins of forlorn Grace Dieu' lying beneath 'yon eastern ridge, the craggy bound, rugged and high, of Charnwood's forest ground.' Grace Dieu Priory was a small and rather poor Augustinian nunnery founded in the thirteenth century. After its dissolution by Henry VIII in 1539, it was converted into a residence by the new landowners and therefore the present scanty remains are a rather jumbled mixture of medieval priory and Tudor house. After years of neglect and inaccessibility, the priory ruins have been recently restored and made the focal point of a nature trail.

Go through the gate to enter the delightful Grace Dieu Wood. If you wish to inspect the priory ruins more closely, immediately turn left through a gate and walk along a track. The route continues ahead through the wood, following the regular Grace Dieu Trail signs. After going under a bridge, turn right and when you see another bridge on the right, a brief detour under the arch leads to the Bulls Head in Thringstone. Otherwise continue winding through the trees and the path eventually emerges onto a road. Turn sharp left along a tree-lined lane, turn right at a junction **6** and at a public footpath sign, turn left over a stile.

Head gently uphill along a fence-lined path and climb a stile to re-enter Cademan Wood. The path curves right through the trees to join another path. Turn left, here rejoining the outward route, and retrace your steps through the wood to the start, looking out for the regular waymarks.

17

From Opencast Mine to Forest Park

Sence Valley

In such pleasant and quiet surroundings it is hard to believe that much of this route is across countryside only recently reclaimed from industry and mining. There is much historic interest, notably the medieval manor house at Donington le Heath and the tiny Norman church at Snibston.

Distance: 7½ miles/12.1km.
Approximate time: 4 hours.
Start: Sence Valley Forest Park, off A447 half a mile (800m) north of Ibstock (GR SK404113).
Maps: Explorer 245; Landranger 128/129.
Car Parking: Free car parks at Sence Valley Forest Park.
Public Transport: Buses from Coalville and Hinckley.
Terrain: Lanes, field paths and tracks; just a few gentle gradients.
Refreshments: Pub at Donington le Heath, café at Donington le Heath Manor House, pub at Ravenstone.
Public Toilets: At start.

Between 1982 and 1996 Sence Valley Forest Park was a vast opencast mining site. Since the end of mining operations, the planting of nearly 100,000 trees by the Forestry Commission has completely transformed the landscape and created an attractive recreational environment. The park was opened in 1998 and comprises 150 acres of woodland, lakes and grassland with fine views.

Start by walking back towards the road ❶, not on the drive but along the parallel path to the left of it. The path turns left through a fence gap and later through another one to a track. Turn right, cross the A447 and, at a public byway sign, keep ahead along a track across fields.

At a footpath post, bear left across a field to another post, go through a hedge gap and keep in the same direction across a field to the next post. Again go through a hedge gap, descend into the next field and head diagonally across it to the far left hand corner. Bear right through a hedge gap, continue along the left edge of a succession of fields, going through a series of hedge gaps, and finally climb a stile onto a road.

The striking Noon Column sculpture in Sence Valley Forest Park
(see p. 34)

Turn left, pass between the supports of a former railway bridge, and follow the road into Donington le Heath. Turn left beside the Corner Pin pub and head gently uphill through the village to the manor house.

The manor house at Donington le Heath is a late thirteenth century stone-built house, modernised and renovated in the seventeenth century. During its long history it has been owned by many families. One of the most

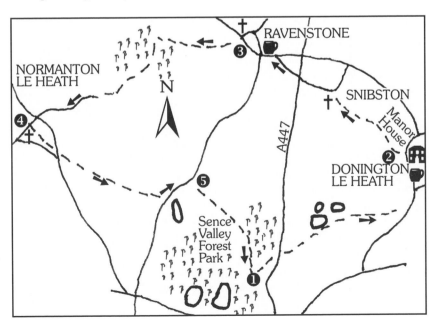

Medieval manor house at Donington le Heath

illustrious of these was the Digbys who lost the house and surrounding lands in the Wars of the Roses but subsequently regained them, probably because Sir John Digby backed the right horse by fighting on the side of Henry Tudor at the battle of Bosworth in 1485. A later member of the family, Everard Digby, brother of the owner of Donington, was one of a number of people executed in 1605 for being involved in the Gunpowder Plot.

By the late seventeenth century the manor house had come into the possession of the Harleys who set up a trust. For the next 300 years it was rented out and used for a variety of purposes, including a pigsty. By the 1960s it was in a very bad state but in 1965 it was bought by Leicestershire County Council and subsequently restored as a period house. The seventeenth century gardens were restored at the same time. The house possesses a fine collection of seventeenth century furniture.

Where the road bends right by the manor house, turn left **2** along Berry Hill Lane and at a public footpath sign, turn right along a left field edge. Go through a hedge gap, turn left to cut across the corner of the next field and continue along its left edge to a stile. Climb it, walk along the right field edge and continue along an enclosed track. The track passes between farm buildings and continues gently uphill to emerge onto the corner of a lane to the right of Snibston church.

The tiny twelfth century church at Snibston stands in rural isolation away from the mining communities that grew up around Coalville during the Industrial Revolution. It is one of the smallest churches in the country.

Keep ahead along the lane to a main road on the edge of Ravenstone. Cross over, take the road ahead (Jennys Lane) and bear left on joining another road. At a crossroads just beyond the pub, turn right along Main Street to the church and turn left into Hospital Lane.

The red sandstone Ravenstone church dates mainly from the fourteenth century. Nearby in Hospital Lane there are some attractive, brick-built almshouses.

At a T-junction ❸ cross the road, climb a stile opposite ands walk along an enclosed path. After climbing the next stile, continue across a field, climb another stile and turn right and left to keep along a right field edge. Climb a stile in the corner and walk along the left edge of the next field towards woodland.

On the edge of the wood, turn right through a hedge gap and turn left onto a track that runs along the right inside edge of the trees. At a public bridleway sign, turn left to continue along another track, initially along the right inside edge of the wood. The track later becomes a hedge-lined, winding track – look out for a right bend – which eventually emerges onto a lane. Turn left into Normanton le Heath, cross a road and continue along the lane opposite to the church.

There is a genuinely remote feel about the small, quiet village of Normanton le Heath. The spire of the thirteenth century church can be seen for miles around across the predominantly flat terrain. Look out for the gargoyles at the top of the west tower.

At a public footpath sign by the church ❹ turn left through a gate, walk along the left edge of the churchyard and climb a stile. Continue along the left edge of a field, descending into a dip, crossing a footbridge and heading up again. Climb a stile in the corner, keep ahead through an area of scrub and trees and bear slightly right across grass to another stile. After climbing it, bear right across the next field and in the corner go through a hedge gap onto a road.

Cross over, walk across the verge, climb a waymarked stile and keep ahead diagonally across a field to a waymarked post by a solitary tree. Go through a hedge gap and continue along the left edge of a succession of fields, going through a series of hedge gaps. In the corner of the third field, continue through bushes to climb a stile, cross a footbridge and turn left along the left edge of the next field. At the next waymarked post, turn right and follow a worn path across the field. Go through a gap on the far side and walk along the right field edge to emerge onto a road.

Turn left downhill and then up again and at a public byway sign, turn right onto a track. ❺ Keep along it for just over half a mile (800m), later heading uphill, and at a footpath sign Birthday Walk, turn right through a fence gap. Walk along a track, go through another fence gap, keep ahead and the track leads back to the car park.

18

Home of the Nine Day Queen

Bradgate Park and Swithland Wood.

This is a classic walk of superb and varied scenery that takes you through a medieval deer park, a beautiful area of woodland and a picturesque village with an old church and thatched cottages. From the higher points there are outstanding views over Charnwood Forest and the surrounding Leicestershire countryside. Within the park are the atmospheric remains of Bradgate House, home of Lady Jane Grey, the 'Nine Day Queen'.

Distance: 8 miles/12.9km
Approximate Time: 4 hours
Start: Newtown Linford, entrance to Bradgate Park, GR SK524098
Maps: Explorer 246; Landranger 129.
Car Parking: Bradgate Park (pay and display)
Public Transport: Buses from Leicester and Loughborough
Terrain: Clear paths and tracks through parkland, woodland and across fields; one stretch across a golf course; modest ascents and descents
Refreshments: Pubs and cafes at Newtown Linford, café at information centre in Bradgate Park, pub on road up to Woodhouse Eaves and pubs at Woodhouse Eaves.
Public Toilets: At start and at three other places within Bradgate Park

---

For centuries *Newtown Linford was part of the Bradgate estate. It is an attractive village with a number of thatched and slate-roofed cottages. The church, situated at the gates of the park, was originally a small and simple structure but was enlarged towards the end of the nineteenth century when the village started to expand.*

❶ Begin by going through the gates into Bradgate Park and walk along the tarmac track beside the little River Lin. After about three-quarters of a mile (1.2km) you pass the remains of Bradgate House on the left and a little further on Bradgate Park Visitor Centre and Cropston Reservoir on the right.

In 1928 the current owner, Charles Bennion, presented Bradgate Park to the people of Leicester and Leicestershire as an area of public recreation and enjoyment. Given its proximity to the city of Leicester – only about six miles away – and its herds of deer, it is an extremely popular spot, especially on fine weekends and bank holidays. This rare example of a largely unaltered and unspoilt medieval deer park was carved out of Charnwood Forest in the thirteenth century and mainly comprises heathland, grassland and bracken dotted with some magnificent ancient oaks and outcrops of granite. The latter give it a rugged appearance which contrasts strongly with the more usual gentler landscapes of Leicestershire.

For most of its history the park was owned by the Grey family and around 1499 Sir Thomas Grey, Marquis of Dorset, began the building of the house, whose redbrick ruins can be seen. Its chief claim to fame is that it was the home of Lady Jane Grey, queen for just nine days in 1553. She was the unwilling figurehead of an unsuccessful attempt by Protestant nobles to prevent the Catholic Mary Tudor from becoming queen. The unfortunate girl paid the price by being subsequently executed. In 1740 Bradgate House was abandoned by the Greys, after which it fell into disrepair.

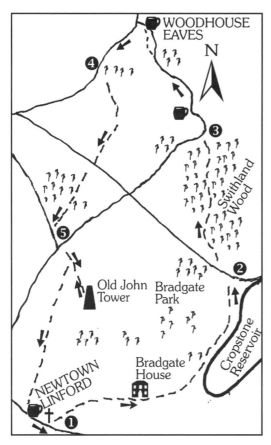

At the far end of the park go through gates onto a road. ❷ Turn left and at a public footpath sign to Swithland Wood, bear right over a stile and walk diagonally across a field towards the edge of the wood. Climb a stile to enter the wood, turn left along its left inside edge and just before reaching a bridge, bear right to a track. Turn right and follow this track in a straight line through the trees. At a fork take the right hand track and shortly after passing through a small clearing and by a Horse Track post, take the left hand path at another fork. The path keeps by the right inside edge of the wood and at the next fork, take the right hand path to reach a road. ❸

Swithland Wood, a surviving remnant of Charnwood Forest, is a beautiful area of mixed woodland, mainly comprising oak, ash, lime, birch, alder and holly. Like Bradgate Park it was given to the city of Leicester. The remains of quarry workings in the wood are an indication that Swithland slate was much prized locally as a roofing material.

Turn right and at a T-junction turn left. Follow the road around a right bend and take the first road on the left, signposted to Woodhouse Eaves. After half a mile (0.8km) and just after a right bend, turn left along an enclosed tarmac track – there is a Cycle Way sign here. At a public footpath sign, turn right through a gate and walk along the left edge of a grassy area. Go through a kissing gate and continue along an enclosed path, heading downhill and bending right. Pass beside a gate and continue down a stony track to rejoin the road in Woodhouse Eaves.

Newton Linford Church

Turn left and turn left again along Maplewell Road. After half a mile (0.8km) and just after a slight right curve, turn left ❹ along a track – this is just in front of a house – heading gently downhill. The track bends right and where it bends left, keep ahead over a stile and walk along the right edge of a field. Climb a stile and turn left along the left edge of the next field. Follow the edge to the right and in the next corner, turn left over a stile.

The next part of the route is across a golf course but it is well-signed. Turn right along the right edge of the course and look out for where a footpath post directs you to turn left to continue by a hedge on the right. Keep an eye out for the regular waymarks as you curve right between two greens, go through a hedge gap and curve right again through trees. At the next footpath post, turn left and keep in a straight line across the course to another belt of trees. Continue in a straight line and go through a gate onto a road.

After going through the gate opposite, continue across another part of the golf course. Pass through a belt of trees, keep ahead and go through a gate on

The ruins of Bradgate House

the far side. Now the way continues steadily uphill across a mixed plantation to emerge onto a road. Turn left and at a T-junction **5** keep ahead through a car park, continue along a wooded track to a kissing gate and go through, here re-entering Bradgate Park. The route continues to the right but a short detour ahead, climbing up to the superb viewpoint of Old John Tower is well worth while.

Ancient oaks in Bradgate Park

Old John Tower is a folly, built by a member of the Grey family in 1784. The views from here are both extensive and magnificent.

Return to the gate that admitted you to the park and turn left along a path that keeps by the park wall on the right, curving gradually left and heading gently downhill. Old John Tower and the war memorial to the Leicestershire Regiment can be seen to the left and there are fine views to the right over the wooded slopes of Charnwood Forest. When you are in line with a clump of trees over to the left (Elder Plantation), turn right through a kissing gate in the boundary wall and walk along the right edge of a field. Bear right to climb a stile in the corner, continue downhill along the right edge of the next field, climb another stile at the bottom and keep ahead to a road.

Turn left through Newtown Linford, passing a number of picturesque thatched cottages. At a sign to Bradgate Park, turn left to return to the car park.

19

Views Across the Water

Thornton Reservoir and Stanton under Bardon

As with several other walks in this guide, it takes quite an effort of the imagination to visualise the surrounding pleasant landscape of green fields, peaceful woodlands, new plantations and reservoir as being scarred by coal mines and pit heaps but this was the case until fairly recently. The route takes in a number of young woods planted through The National Forest project and there are a series of fine views both across Thornton Reservoir and over the Leicestershire countryside.

Distance: 5 miles/8km.
Approximate time: 2½ hours.
Start: Thornton Reservoir (GR SK471075).
Maps: Explorer 245; Landranger 129/140.
Car Parking: Free Severn Trent Water car park at Thornton Reservoir.
Public Transport: Buses from Leicester and Coalville.
Terrain: Apart from waterside paths at the start and finish, most of the walking is along field and woodland paths with some fairly gentle gradients.
Refreshments: Pubs at Thornton, garden centre cafe by car park entrance, pub at Stanton under Bardon.
Public Toilets: By reservoir just after start of walk.

Unlike *Staunton Harold, the 75-acre Thornton Reservoir has been in existence for a long time. It was constructed in 1854 but only made available to the general public in 1997. Since then it has become a popular centre for birdwatchers, anglers, cyclists and walkers.*

Facing the reservoir ❶, turn left along the tarmac path beside it, passing the information centre and toilet block. Shortly afterwards turn left, at a public footpath sign, through a gate and head uphill along a path which bends right and continues along the right edge of Thornton churchyard. Pass beside the lych gate onto a road and keep ahead to a T-junction in Thornton.

Thornton was initially an agricultural settlement on the fringes of Charnwood Forest and later became a mining village. The fine thirteenth century church has an impressive spire.

Looking across Thornton Reservoir

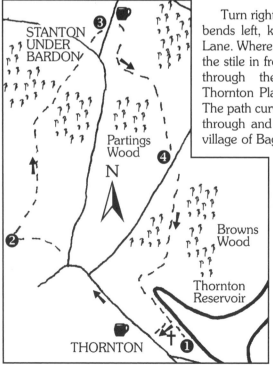

Turn right and where the main road bends left, keep ahead along Stanton Lane. Where the lane bends right, climb the stile in front and walk along a path through the young woodland of Thornton Plantation, planted in 1998. The path curves left to a hedge gap. Go through and walk across a field – the village of Bagworth can be seen on the ridge ahead – to a footpath post on the far side. ❷ At this point turn sharp right and follow a path gently uphill across the same field, making for the far left hand corner.

Go through a wide hedge gap and turn left along the left edge of the next field, keeping in line with the electricity pylons. At a waymarked stile by another wide hedge gap the path divides. Take the right hand path, heading diagonally across the field to a stile. Climb it and turn left along the left edge of another area of recently planted woodland.

This new wood, planted as recently as 2002-03, is called Partings Wood and the name has an interesting derivation. It is situated approximately half way between the villages of Thornton and Stanton under Bardon and courting couples allegedly used to part here when walking each other home.

Turn right at the corner of the wood to continue along its right edge and turn left over a stile. Head downhill across a field to a stile, climb it and go through the squeezer stile immediately in front onto a lane. Climb the stile opposite, head uphill along the right edge of two fields, climbing another stile, and in the top corner of the second field turn right over a stile. Walk along an enclosed path, climb a stile and continue to a lane on the edge of Stanton under Bardon. ❸

As its name indicates Stanton is situated below Bardon Hill, which at 912 feet (278m) is the highest hill in Leicestershire. It was a quarrying village and the hill has been extensively quarried for its distinctive greenish rock, a kind of granite, since as early as 1622.

Turn left, almost immediately turn right beside the pub along Meadow Lane and at a public footpath sign, bear right along a tarmac track to a waymarked gate. Go through, continue along a track between houses and look out for where you turn right to a waymarked gate – this could easily be missed. Go through, head gently downhill by a hedge on the right, climb a stile and walk across a field to a stile on the far side.

Climb it onto a road but immediately turn left over another stile and walk along the left edge of a field. In the corner turn right to continue along the edge, climb a stile and keep along the left edge of a plantation, part of Partings Wood again. At the corner of the wood, cross a footbridge, keep ahead and go through a gate onto a road.

Turn right and at a public footpath sign, turn left through a hedge gap ❹ and walk along the left edge of The National Forest plantation of Ashley's Wood. Turn right at a waymarked post to continue through the trees, climb a stile – here leaving the wood – and keep ahead along the right edge of a field. Climb a stile just to the left of the corner and continue in a straight line gently downhill through Browns Wood. Go through a hedge gap and keep ahead to a waymarked post.

Turn left over a footbridge, turn right and where the path divides at a junction just ahead, take the left hand waymarked path. Climb a stile on the edge of the trees – there is a fine view ahead of the reservoir and spire of Thornton church – turn right along a right field edge and go through a kissing gate onto a track. Turn right and cross an outlet stream at the end of the reservoir. The track curves left and continues beside the water back to the start.

20

Death of a King

Bosworth Battlefield

Starting from the top of Ambion Hill, a superb viewpoint, most of the route is across the battlefield of Bosworth and part of it follows a well-signed Battle Trail that has regular information boards. Although the terrain has changed much since the time of the battle in 1485 – the most obvious additions are the railway, canal and Ambion Wood – Bosworth is one of the best preserved battle sites in England and it is still possible, with a little imagination, to follow the course of the conflict.

Distance: 4 miles/6.4km.
Approximate time: 2 hours.
Start: Bosworth Battlefield Visitor Centre, signposted from A447 and other roads near Market Bosworth (GR SK402001).
Maps: Explorer 232; Landranger 140.
Car Parking: Pay car park at Bosworth Battlefield.
Public Transport: None.
Terrain: Easy walking along mostly well-surfaced paths and a canal towpath.
Refreshments: Café at Visitor Centre, canalside café at Sutton Wharf.
Public Toilets: At start and at Shenton Station.

By any criteria Bosworth ranks as one of the most significant battles in English history. It was virtually the final battle of the long Wars of the Roses, ushered in the powerful Tudor dynasty and is widely regarded as marking the end of the Middle Ages. It was also the last occasion on which an English king was killed in battle. It was fought between Richard III and Henry Tudor and at stake was the throne of England.

Richard III had come to the throne two years before in highly dubious circumstances. In that year his brother Edward IV died at an early age and his successor, Edward V, was a boy of only 12. Richard, then Duke of Gloucester and the young king's uncle, acted as regent and arranged for Edward and his younger brother, Richard Duke of York, to be conveyed to the Tower of London. Richard then had himself crowned king and the two 'Princes in the Tower' later mysteriously disappeared. Not surprisingly such action aroused much hostility and discontent among the nobility and Henry Tudor Earl of

Richmond, a Welshman and currently in exile in France, became the focal point of opposition to Richard.

Henry landed in Pembrokeshire on 7 August 1485 and marched across Wales and into the Midlands. Richard was based at Nottingham Castle. He moved to Leicester and the two armies met near Market Bosworth. The battle

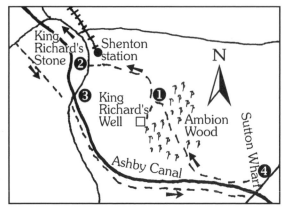

was fought on 22 August. Richard had the advantage of occupying the top of Ambion Hill, the starting point of the walk, and had a larger and more experienced army but, because of his widespread unpopularity, some of his supporters were lukewarm. The turning point in the battle came when the powerful Stanleys threw their 4000 troops behind Henry. After fierce fighting, Richard was defeated and killed and Henry Tudor ascended the throne as Henry VII, first of the Tudor monarchs.

The visitor centre has more information about the battle, plus books, gifts, models and displays. In addition a full sized, replica medieval village, Ambion Parva, has been reconstructed on the site.

Start in front of the visitor centre ❶ and take the path signposted 'Battle Trail and Shenton Station'. At a T-junction, a short detour to the left, then turning right through a hedge gap brings you to King Richard's Well.

Richard III is supposed to have slaked his thirst from the spring here during the battle. It is now topped by a stone pyramid.

Return to the T-junction, keep ahead over the crest of the hill and follow the path around right and left bends. Despite its modest height, 354 feet (120m), Ambion Hill is a fine vantage point and from here there are grand views looking ahead over open and gently undulating country

King Richard's Well

Looking towards Market Bosworth from Ambion Hill

towards Market Bosworth. Head downhill by a hedge on the right, curving left and then continuing down an enclosed path. Go through two gates in quick succession and keep ahead to Shenton station.

The station is one of the termini on the Battlefield Line. The trains, both steam-hauled and diesel, run from here to Shackerstone where there is a museum, shop and café.

Cross the railway line, bear right across the station car park to a road and turn right. ❷ A parallel path to the left of the road leads into King Richard's Field.

The memorial stone in the field by the stream marks the place near where Richard was allegedly killed in the battle.

Return to the road, continue along it and take the first road on the left, signposted to Shenton and Sibson, passing under an aqueduct. At a public footpath sign, turn left through a gate, walk in a straight line across a field studded with trees, cross a footbridge over a stream, keep ahead and go through a gate onto a lane. Turn left towards the canal bridge and at a public footpath sign to Ashby Canal, bear slightly right along an enclosed path and turn right onto the towpath. ❸

The Ashby Canal was built between 1794 and 1804 and linked the coalmines around Moira and Ashby with the Coventry Canal near Nuneaton. It declined after the coming of the railways and this, coupled with instability caused by mining subsidence, led to its closure in the 1940s. Some of the northern industrial part has disappeared but this southerly, more agricultural section has survived and is a popular recreational amenity, passing through much unspoilt and pleasant countryside.

Now comes a very attractive stretch of canalside walking to Sutton Wharf, a distance of 1¼ miles (2km). At Bridge 34 climb steps onto the road, turn left over the bridge and turn left again through a gate into Sutton Wharf car park. ❹ Continue along the other side of the canal, go through a kissing gate and keep ahead to enter Ambion Wood.

King Richard's Stone

Although it occupies part of the battle site, Ambion Wood did not exist in 1485. The terrain then comprised open grassy slopes.

The path curves right through the trees to a kissing gate on the edge of the wood. Go through, walk across a field, go through another kissing gate and keep ahead to the start.

The Ashby Canal

Index

More walks from the Meridian catalogue

RAMBLERS' CHOICE: Some favourite walks in the Midlands. Edited by Peter Groves

In this collection members of the City of Birmingham Group of the Ramblers' Association offer some of their favourite walks in Warwickshire, West Midlands, Worcestershire and Staffordshire. They are not too difficult and many have longer and shorter versions, the longer walks ranging from about 5 miles/8km to 9½ miles/15 km; the shorter walks from about 3 miles/5 km to 7¾ miles/12.5 km.

£5.95. ISBN 978-1-869922-54-2. 96 pages. 31 illustrations. 20 maps

HERITAGE DISCOVERY WALKS IN THE MIDLANDS by Peter Groves

Britain has a rich historical heritage and the twenty-one walks in this book explore some fine Midlands countryside and also present opportunities to visit castles, battlefields, nature reserves, museums, churches and cathedrals, to admire fine architecture and to explore some historic towns. The walks range from 2½ miles/4km to 11¼ miles/18 km.

£6.95. ISBN 1-869922-50-6. 160 pages. 52 illustrations. 20 maps

A YEAR OF WALKS IN THE THREE CHOIRS COUNTIES by Roy Woodcock

The Three Choirs Counties comprise Herefordshire, Gloucestershire and Worcestertshire and this selection of walks takes twelve widely distributed locations, one for each month of the year.

£6.95. ISBN 1-869922-51-4. 112 pages. 28 illustrations. 12 maps

WALKS IN SEVERN COUNTRY by Roy Woodcock

The River Severn, Britain's longest river, rises on the slopes of Plynlimon in Wales and flows through the beautiful counties of Powys, Shropshire, Worcestershire and Gloucestershire before discharging into the Bristol Channel. In this book the author presents twenty walks that explore some of the fine towns and countryside that the Severn passes through on its 220 mile journey to the sea.

£7.95. ISBN 1-869922-49-2. 128 pages. 37 illustrations. 20 maps

WALKS IN SEVERN COUNTRY by Roy Woodcock

The River Severn, Britain's longest river, rises on the slopes of Plynlimon in Wales and flows through the beautiful counties of Powys, Shropshire, Worcestershire and Gloucestershire before discharging into the Bristol Channel. In this book the author presents an absorbing account of the geography and history of the river accompanied by twenty walks that explore some of the fine towns and countryside that the Severn passes through on its 220 mile journey to the sea. Distances range from two to twelve miles, with an average of about six miles.

£7.95. ISBN 1-869922-49-2. 128 pages. 37 illustrations. 20 maps

WALKS THROUGH HISTORY IN THE HEART OF ENGLAND by Roger Seedhouse

The Heart of England is rich in history, both ancient and more modern, and the twenty-four walks in this book will offer the enquiring walker many intriguing glimpses of a bygone age – with iron-age forts, battle sites, medieval castles and even a second world war camp. All of them start at, or pass through, places of historical interest that will add greatly to your appreciation of a day out in beautiful walking country.

£8.95 ISBN 1-869922-41-7. 160 pages. 38 photos. 24 maps.

WALKS TO WET YOUR WHISTLE by Roger Seedhouse

Eighteen walks covering some of the most beautiful countryside in Shropshire and along its Staffordshire borders, each providing an opportunity to visit a pub in which the walker will feel welcome and comfortable.

£6.95. ISBN 1 869922 41 7. 112 pages. 17 photographs. 18 maps.

MORE WALKS TO WET YOUR WHISTLE by Roger Seedhouse

A second collection of walks with a pub in Shropshire and along its Staffordshire borders.

£6.95. ISBN 1 869922 36 0. 112 pages. 24 photographs. 18 maps.

WARWICKSHIRE WALKS TO WET YOUR WHISTLE by Roger Seedhouse

Roger Seedhouse's third collection of walks, all with good pubs, in Warwickshire – a land of lakes and country parks which are a delight to behold, merging into the Northern Cotswolds with its buildings of honey-hued stone.

£8.95. ISBN 1-869922-48-4 120 pages 21 photos 20 maps

WALKING WITH THE FAMOUS ... AND THE INFAMOUS by Roger Seedhouse

A unique book of fifteen walks in Shropshire through areas associated with some of the county's most colourful historical characters. In an original and distinctive style the walks also relate the principal events of the character's lives and are written as if through their own eyes.

£7.95. ISBN 1-869922-46-8. 128 pages. 15 maps. Illustrated with photos and drawings.

**WALKS IN SOUTH WARWICKSHIRE
FROM SHAKESPEARE COUNTRY TO THE COTSWOLDS** by John W Parnham and Barry R Wills

This collection of circular walks represent the authors' favourites within this lovely, varied region. The walks will take you along ancient trackways and paths, past standing stones, earthworks, country estates and grand houses. In the Arden countryside as well as finding connections to William Shakespeare you will discover hidden valleys and distinct wooded hilltops that offer wonderful views. Further south the walks will take you through delightful villages and into remote areas in the Cotswold Hills that rival in many ways the better known parts of this beautiful region.

£6.95. ISBN 1 869922 38 7. 112 pages. 36 sketches. 18 maps.

WALKS IN WARWICKSHIRE AND WORCESTERSHIRE A Third Collection by Des Wright

This third collection of walks by a popular author explores further some of the attractive countryside in two West Midlands counties. The walking is not difficult, mostly on the flat and with no strenuous climbs. The walks are all circular and can be reached easily by car and, with one exception, by public transport. Distances range between 2 and 9.5 miles, with one rather more strenuous walk of l4 miles.

£6.95. ISBN 1-869922-44-1. 112 pages. 24 illustrations. 22 maps.

Long Distance Walks

THE MONARCH'S WAY by Trevor Antill

A long distance walk that closely follows the route taken by Charles II after his defeat by Cromwell's forces at Worcester in 1651. Starting from Worcester it goes first north, then south through the Cotswolds and the Mendips to the coast, then along the South Downs to Shoreham where Charles escaped to France.

Book 1: Worcester to Stratford-upon-Avon. 180 miles.Revised second edition £6.95. ISBN 1 869922 52 2. 112 pages. 19 photographs, 8 drawings, 19 maps.

Book 2: Stratford-upon-Avon to Charmouth. 210 miles.£6.95. ISBN 1 869922 28 X. 136 pages. 21 photographs. 23 maps.

Book 3: Charmouth to Shoreham. 225 miles. £6.95. ISBN 1 869922 29 8. 136 pages. 21 photographs. 25 maps.

THE ELAN VALLEY WAY by David Milton

The Elan Valley Way runs from Frankley, on the western fringe of Birmingham, to the Elan Valley in mid-Wales. It is loosely based around the course followed by the Elan Valley aqueduct along which Birmingham's water supply has passed since 1904. Largely following footpaths and bridleways, and with many superb views, the 128½ mile route passes through some delightful walking areas in the counties of Worcestershire, Shropshire, Herefordshire and Powys.

£7.95. ISBN 1 869922 39 5. 160 pages. 21 photographs. 21 maps.

A TEME VALLEY WALK by David Milton

The Teme is one of the most beautiful and fast-flowing rivers in the country but remains quite secretive for much of its length. This long distance walk remains as close as possible to the river but takes to the hills where footpaths, public transport or accommodation needs dictate. It starts in Worcester and ends, after visiting the source of the river, in Newtown, a total distance of 93 miles.

£8.95. ISBN 1-869922-45-X. 176 pages. 22 illustrations. 17 maps.

THE RIVERSIDES WAY by David Milton

A 70 mile circular walk in the area of the Welsh Marches immediately to the south and west of Ludlow. Centred on Aymestry it takes in the valleys and surrounding hills of the two rivers that drain the region – the Teme, in the north, and the Lugg, in the south.

£8.95. ISBN 1-869922-43-3. 160 pages. 13 photos. 14 maps.

THE NAVIGATION WAY: A Hundred Mile Towpath Walk by Peter Groves and Trevor Antill

Starting from the centre of Birmingham and encompassing fourteen West Midlands canals the Navigation Way follows a meandering course through varied urban areas and delightful countryside until terminating at Chasewater. The book also contains ten additional circular 'canal-link' walks in some of the attractive walking areas adjacent to the canals.

Third revised edition.£5.95. ISBN 1 869922 35 2. 112 pages. 34 photographs. 24 maps.

All Meridian titles are available from booksellers or, if in difficulty, direct from the publishers.

Please send your remittance, including the following amounts for postage and packing:
Order value up to £10.00 add £1.50;
over £10.00 and up to £20.00 add £2.50;
over £20.00 add £3.00.

Meridian Books Sales Office
8 Hartside Close, Lutley, Halesowen, West Midlands B63 1HP
Tel: 0121-429 4397
e-mail: meridian.books@tiscali.co.uk

Please send for our complete catalogue of walking guides.